THE ULTIM

Tailgater's™

RACING GUIDE

STEPHEN LINN

[interactive blvd]™

An Interactive Blvd Book
interactiveblvd.com

RUTLEDGE HILL PRESS®
Nashville, Tennessee

A Division of Thomas Nelson Publishers
www.ThomasNelson.com

theultimatetailgater.com

An Interactive Blvd Book. Interactive Blvd is a division of 4964 Productions, LLC., www.interactiveblvd.com.

Published by Rutledge Hill Press, a Division of Thomas Nelson, Inc., P.O. Box 141000, Nashville, Tennessee 37214.

This book is sold without warranties, expressed or implied, and the publisher and author disclaim any liability for injury, loss, or damage caused by the contents of this book.

Rutledge Hill Press books may be purchased in bulk for educational, business, fundraising, or sales promotional use. For information, please e-mail SpecialMarkets@ThomasNelson.com.

Photos: John F. Motal: 5, 19, 30, 37, 98, 100, 105, 108; Steve Glor: 16, 17; A.R.E. Accessories LLC: 17; Rocket Racing League: 40, 41; DJ Smith: 33 (illustration); Kati Molin: 60; Diane Rutt: 62; Heung Tsang: 66; Marcelo Wain: 68; Carla Lisinski: 72; James Pauls: 78; Andrew Penner: 84; Ryan Scott: 87; Satu Knape: 90, 97; Bill Ox: 93; All other photographs by Ed Rode.

Design by Karen Williams [intudesign.net]

Recipes (excluding Drunken Steaks and Honey-Glazed Pork Chops) courtesy of *American Profile* and printed with permission.

Special thanks to Jenn Brown, Shanon Davis, Terry McMillen, Steve Ney, Barb Rishaw, Jim Walczak, and Karen Williams for all of their help and support.

Library of Congress Cataloging-in-Publication Data

Linn, Stephen, 1964-
  The ultimate tailgater's racing guide / Stephen Linn.
     p. cm.
  ISBN-13: 978-1-4016-0334-2
  ISBN-10: 1-4016-0334-3
  1. Tailgate parties--United States. 2. Outdoor cookery.
3. Entertaining. 4. Racetracks (Automobile racing)--United States. I. Title.

  GV1472.L56 2007
  641.5'78--dc22

Printed in the United States of America

07 08 09 10 11— 5 4 3 2 1

Contents

Tailgating Racing Style

It seems fitting that a sport celebrating the automobile is one of the biggest tailgating attractions in the country.

But before I get too far along, let me be clear about one thing. There are a lot of great books about racing and what happens on the track. This isn't one of them. This book is about what happens *outside* the track. That's where you'll find some of the most passionate fans of any sport in the world.

The first auto race in the United States was in 1895, an event sponsored by the *Chicago Times-Herald*. It was a 54-mile course from Chicago to Evanston and back. Six "horseless carriages" sped through the snow. Okay, maybe "sped" isn't the right word. Inventor J. Frank Duryea won the contest with a time of 10 hours, 23 minutes, and an average speed of about 7 miles per hour. Not exactly Jeff Gordon stats, but he did make history and pocket $2,000 for the victory (equivalent to more than $40,000 in 2007 dollars—not too bad).

That was the first race, but not the first tailgate party.

Historians will tell you the first tailgate party was in 1863 at the Civil War's Battle of Manassas (great concept, bad application—war really isn't the best spectator sport). Tailgating took on its more contemporary setting six years later at a Rutgers/Princeton football game. But it was when people with surnames like Benz, Daimler, and Ford started producing automobiles that America began its love affair with cars and tailgating started down the road to becoming a part of our cultural being. Of course, at the time no one could imagine how the two would later meet at places like Daytona, Darlington, and Richmond.

The automobile allowed us to more easily transport our families, friends, and food to new places. Whether it was the open road or a parking lot, we couldn't wait to drive there. When they first attached tailgates to cars, we were hooked. By the 1970s, wagons with names like Vista Cruiser and Town & Country sported tailgates as big as dining tables. Now we have SUVs almost big enough to hold a Town & Country, and with tailgates customized to hold drinks, plug in a TV, and attach a grill.

For racing fans, the evolution of the RV is just as important, maybe more so. After all, it's as much camping as it is tailgating. Ultimate racing tailgaters pull into the track's parking lots as early as Wednesday or Thursday—and don't leave until Sunday. Stay much longer than that, and you may have to pay property taxes.

The forebears of today's RVs got their start in the 1920s—although it was called "auto camping" then. Private rail cars were the primary inspiration for the house trailers and travel trailers that became popular in the 1930s. Many of these models used aircraft-style construction and offered their owners beds, dinettes, electricity, and water. Pretty cool stuff, since at the time there were still areas of the country where homes didn't have all of that.

After World War II, the industry flourished as Americans took to the open road

Racing tailgaters share a special bond most of their football tailgating cousins don't. The sense of community among racing tailgaters runs as deep as their feelings about Jeff Gordon and Dale Earnhardt, Funny Cars, and Top Fuel dragsters.

Today, if you want to see the variety of styles and amenities of the modern RV, don't go to a showroom— go to a race track.

in larger numbers. And while it was coincidental, RVs grew in size and popularity alongside NASCAR, which got its start in 1948.

Today, if you want to see the variety of styles and amenities of the modern RV, don't go to a showroom—go to Talladega, or Bristol, or Pocono.

Racing tailgaters—whether in RVs, tents, or the backseats of their cars—share a special bond most of their football tailgating cousins don't. The sense of community among racing tailgaters runs as deep as their feelings about Jeff Gordon and Dale Earnhardt, Funny Cars, and Top Fuel dragsters. For many, it runs deeper. There are life-long friendships forged in these parking-lot neighborhoods. After all, camp with someone for a few days and you really get to know them.

And that community feeling doesn't make its home only at NASCAR

ETIQUETTE TIP

#15

Introduce yourself to your tailgate neighbors, and invite them to share a meal with you.

Nextel Cup races. It's just as spirited at the Dodge Weekly race at Corning, Iowa's Adams County Speedway, and the IHRA race at Milan Dragway in Michigan.

This book celebrates these communities. It will also help you throw the best party in the parking lot, with tips on the gear you'll need, recipes, and track guides for nearly 300 venues coast-to-coast.

Of course, there's always more than fits in a book. At theultimatetailgater.com, you'll find more tips, more recipes, podcasts, and tailgating videos.

The Gear

Before a race, drivers and their crews pore over checklists and amass the gear they need for the weekend. You may not need a restrictor plate or trailing arm, but you will need a place to sleep and something to eat.

The type of gear you need—and how much of it—depends on how long you plan to tailgate and how big your wallet is. But the popularity of motorsports means you have more options than ever, and at more price levels than ever. We'll get to checklists in a bit (page 49, to be exact), but before you know what to put on your checklists, you have some decisions to make.

For tailgating at races, your gear falls into three primary categories: sleeping, wearing, and eating. For each category, ask yourself a few basic questions before you start shopping:

1. How many races will I go to each year?
2. How long will I tailgate at each race?
3. What will the weather be like?
4. Will I have a way to power a refrigerator?
5. Is the track close to any towns or stores where I can get supplies during the weekend?
6. What's my budget?

The answers to these questions will decide whether you go with a tent or an RV, with shorts or parkas, with gas or charcoal.

Sleeping

TENTS

One of the things I find interesting when talking with tailgaters at races around the country is how many of them started their tailgating "careers" in tents. Even folks who today sit in fancy RVs and buses often camped at their first few races in tents.

Why not? Compared to a trailer or RV, tents are dirt cheap (pun partially intended). Plus, if you're not sure how much you'll like multiday tailgating, a tent is a smart way to try it out. Depending on the type of tent you get, you'll probably spend $200 to $500.

Of course, you'll probably miss some of the amenities other camping options offer (like a bathroom and running water), but if you pick the right spot, offer enough food and drinks, and ask real nicely, you may be able to at least use your neighbor's bathroom.

There are a few things to keep in mind when tent shopping. First, chances are you're not hiking to Bristol, so don't worry as much about the weight of your tent as the stability and sturdiness of it. Be sure to pick a tent that will withstand the harshest conditions you might encounter. I can't tell you how many people tell me stories about the year it snowed or was 30 degrees, and they froze because they had only a tarp shelter.

Compared to a trailer or RV, tents are dirt cheap.

When shopping, you'll find three-season and four-season tents. The former is for spring, summer, and fall in temperate climates. The latter is for all year in most any climate. You'll also have your choice of materials,

At some warm-weather races, people set up basic screen shelters and call it a night.

usually polyester (holds up well in the sun), nylon (lighter weight), and canvas (durable, but heavy). In addition to the material, be sure to look at the stitching. Most discount tents have fewer stitches per inch, and often they don't have seam sealing.

You'll also have a choice of aluminum poles and fiberglass poles; the better tents tend to use aluminum.

While you're shopping, it's worth your time to look at freestanding tents—especially if you think you may move around some looking for the best spot. These tents stand without using stakes, and in addition to being relatively portable, they're pretty easy to shake out when you're ready to pack it up and head home.

Another factor in your decision is how many people will be using your tent. If your tailgate crew has four or more, take a look at family tents (sometimes called basecamp tents). But don't just look at the capacity ratings before buying—look at the tent set up. I don't know who estimates how many people can fit into a tent, but I think it's a short, skinny guy. It may say "sleeps six," but if all six are large adults, and you have any gear inside, you may unexpectedly find yourselves becoming even closer friends if you don't set up the tent and check first.

Many tailgaters expand their tents with awnings and other accessories, including sleep screens and tarps. In fact, at some warm-weather races, I've seen people set up basic screen shelters and call it a night. Just keep in mind these simpler shelters may keep you from the bugs, but not the rain.

RVS

There's a reason you see so many RVs at tracks across the country. After all, tailgating with an RV means you can easily take your tailgate setup with you anywhere, and it offers many of the comforts of home—like the bathroom the guy in the tent will be asking to use.

The type of RV you want is based in large part on the type of tailgater you are and if you'll use your RV for more than just tailgating. You'll find everything from truck campers for weekenders to travel trailers to motorhomes suitable for rock stars. How do you know if you're a weekender or a rock star? Besides the whole can-you-sing thing, ask yourself these questions:

1. Will I use my RV for a couple of races or for traveling all year?
2. Will I be making long trips?
3. How many people will sleep in it?
4. How much storage room do I need for my tailgating gear?
5. How much, and what type, of cooking will I do?
6. Will I have an entertainment center?
7. Do I need to tow a car?
8. What's my budget?

How you answer those questions will help you decide what type of RV is best for you.

ETIQUETTE TIP

#27

Leave your tailgate space the way you found it.

TRUCK CAMPER

These are the units that fit onto a pickup truck. They are an economical choice and a practical choice for people who may tailgate at just a few races each year (especially if you already have the pickup).

Most of these units can sleep four and come with jacks so you can detach it, set it up in your tailgate space, and then have use of your pickup. When looking at truck campers, check out amenities like a bathroom, a shower, some sort of kitchen, and air conditioner units.

If you can afford it (these campers will run you about $12,000 and up), you may want to get one with pop-up roofs or slide-outs to increase your living area.

FOLDING CAMPING TRAILER

These trailers are 15 to 20 feet long and can be had for just a few thousand dollars. Depending on the model, they can sleep up to eight people and include a kitchen area with a stove and refrigerator. Some models also have bathrooms.

Truck campers are an economical and practical choice for people who tailgate at just a few races each year.

This lightweight trailer can be pulled by almost any vehicle, including many compact cars. And unlike its larger siblings, it's light enough that you can unhook it and maneuver it by hand into tight spaces. (Plus, picking up a trailer and moving it by hand is a great way to impress a date; just don't mention the whole "lightweight" thing.)

Folding camper trailers are lightweight and can be pulled by almost any vehicle.

Of course, like any trailer, it can't drive itself, so you'll have two vehicles to park, which can get tricky at some tracks that have smaller spaces or don't allow you to park the towing vehicle overnight in the campground. (Check the Track Guides beginning on page 111 to find out about those restrictions.)

EXPANDABLE TRAVEL TRAILER

This style trailer is a little larger than the folding camping trailer (by 4 or 5 feet) and offers a few more standard amenities. Most models can sleep up to eight people and offer pop-outs for more living area.

They may be bigger, but they are still light enough to be pulled by most midsized cars. Expect to pay closer to $10,000 for one of these.

FIFTH WHEEL TRAVEL TRAILER

In this case, being the fifth wheel is a good thing.

These trailers are towed by pickups or similar vehicles with a special "fifth wheel" hitch. They are one of the most spacious RVs on the road, with taller ceilings and more slide-outs and other amenities than most RVs. Up to eight can sleep comfortably in most models, which also have many of the comforts of home: bathrooms, showers, kitchens, and entertainment centers.

It is bigger (21–40 feet) and more spacious, but it is a trailer so it will take more practice to maneuver; unlike the smaller, lighter trailers, you must take care to match the weight of the fifth wheel travel trailer to the towing capacity of your vehicle.

Travel trailers offer many of the amenities of home and are the most popular RV for general use.

Of course, more room and more amenities mean more money; expect to pay around $20,000 for one of these trailers.

TRAVEL TRAILER

The travel trailer is the most common RV for general use. But many don't look like RVs at all on the inside.

You may still tow them, but some models come with roof-top patios, fireplaces, offices, hide-away beds, full kitchens, and dining areas. Some even come with garages. Really.

Most models sleep up to eight, and the length ranges from 12 to 35 feet. Prices start around $15,000; depending on size and amenities, you can keep adding to the price tag until it empties your wallet. Fireplaces and garages cost money, after all.

CLASS A MOTORHOMES

These gems look more like a bus than an RV, and many have central heat and air, along with baths, showers, kitchens, entertainment centers, several slide-out rooms, and an almost endless list of amenities. You'll pay for them, though. Be ready to shell out $80,000 to $1,000,000 for one of these. (If you get the $1,000,000 model, will you invite me to a race with you . . . please?)

Class A motorhomes are anywhere from 21 to 40 feet long with much of the space being for living and entertainment.

While they're anywhere from 21 to 40 feet long, much of that space is for living and entertainment, so many models sleep up to six people, rather than eight.

CLASS B CAMPER VAN

These RVs may be just 16 to 21 feet long (not that much longer than regular vans), but they fit a lot inside. They usually sleep four, but include a kitchen, bathroom, and shower. You can also stand up in most models since the roof is raised. They

Ultimate Tailgate Trucks

Okay, so about the only place you'll see these trucks is on display at a track or auto show—they're show trucks, after all—but these portable parties will have many tailgaters trying to figure out how to trick out their rides this way.

Most of these vehicles begin life as a regular truck. "Snake-bitten," for example, began life as a Ford F150, but after several months of work, it became a tailgating truck. While it may still look like a Ford F150 on the outside, hidden under the bed top is an A/V system with an LCD television, a gaming system, a cargo management system, coolers, and more. You'll find a Freedom Grill attached to the hitch that swings out so you can cook anywhere, and a satellite dish up top so you can watch TV anywhere.

"Carnivore."

Freedom Grill also tricked out some trucks to showcase its products—and throw a great party. One is a converted pickup with molded grill tool holders in the hitch, a TV under the bed top, and a top-notch stereo system.

But the other—"Carnivore"—will be the hit of an awful lot of parking lots. It opens-up into a complete sports bar with counter tops, multiple televisions, a storage system, a stereo system to rival a dance club, and, of course, a grill.

These makeovers take time—it took about a year to turn Carnivore from basic truck into tailgating monster—and they will separate you from a lot of cash. A whole lot of cash. But when it's finished, you'll have a whole lot of new friends at your tailgate party happy to hang out and watch prerace coverage on your nice, big TV. You're also likely to find that more people will want to take their picture with your truck than with you.

"Snake-bitten" (above).

are so compact that some people use these not only for tailgating, but as their primary vehicle year-round.

However you use it, expect to pay around $60,000 for a new one.

CLASS C MINI MOTORHOME

These motorhomes are the ones that have a bunk hanging over the cab. Probably the most common RVs for tailgaters, they offer the same amenities as most motorhomes—but for less money (expect to pay $50,000 and up). You can sleep up to six in most models, which are 21 to 35 feet long. Inside you'll find a bathroom, shower, and kitchen, and many have slide-outs to offer more living space.

No matter what type of RV you settle on, there are some features you should ask about if they don't come standard:

- A storage area under the floor with enough room to stash your grill, folding tables, chairs, and other supplies
- Air conditioner
- LP furnace
- Hardwired generator
- A video back-up system (they don't have back windows, and you want to see what's behind you)
- An awning (which you will find more than useful for setting up the conversation area for your tailgate party)

Once you arrive at the track, you'll find most have specific camping areas for RVs.

Class C mini motorhomes offer many of the same amenities as larger RV models.

Check the Track Guides (beginning on page 111) for details on those, and it's always wise to check the track's Web site before you leave to see whether there's anything else you should know.

If you find yourself in a bind for a night, most Wal-Marts will let you park RVs overnight for free. It's not a company policy—it's up to each store's manager—but most permit it. Call to be sure, though.

BUSES

There's one other vehicle you see scattered about the lots at races, mostly in the lots alongside the track or in the infield: buses.

Some are expensive custom coaches outfitted with stuff you probably wouldn't mind having in your house. But most are custom buses whose former life was most likely taking kids to Spring Valley Elementary.

Fun tailgating vehicles are the converted, rebuilt, and customized school buses.

Some of the most fun tailgating vehicles are the converted, rebuilt, and customized school buses. Some are gutted and turned into traveling hotel suites. Many are more modest in appointment but show the spirit of the fans who ride in them.

Not only do the buses provide a way to get to the track and a place to sleep, but they also offer height. Look across the infield, just outside the track fences, or along the drag strips, and you'll see platforms on top of these vehicles (as well as atop several RVs) sporting everything from standing-room-only balconies, to chairs, to couches with side tables that border on being elevated living rooms.

If you want to go this route, it's actually cheaper than you might think. At least for the bus (the customization is where you'll drop some cash). A quick search of eBay finds used school buses for as little as $300—but you might want to have that one checked out by a mechanic first.

Wearing

Your tailgate attire needs to be more thought-out than just tossing on an old pair of jeans and a #6 hat. Your outfit will be scrutinized and talked about—from what driver is on your shirt to what color your face paint is.

Not only does what you wear say something about who you are (and who you support), but it can also mean the difference between being comfortable for the next several days or becoming good friends

ETIQUETTE TIP

#109

Always thank the host for inviting you to the tailgate party. Even if the food was bad.

with the track medics. I'm sure they're nice folks, but that's not why you came to the race.

Build your tailgating wardrobe the same way you build your work and casual wardrobes. And I do mean "build" your tailgating wardrobe. Choose pieces that can mix, match, and coordinate during the days you're at the track. Not only will this help you layer up for cool nights (and down for hot days) in proper style, but it will also help prevent you from packing seven suitcases for the trip. Fewer suitcases in the car means more room for food and drinks.

While there are millions of ways to jazz up your racing wardrobe (literally—an Internet search for "NASCAR apparel" turns up about 5 million Web sites), the best way to show your spirit is on outerwear. Jackets, coats, rain ponchos, hats, sweatshirts, and the like will help you dress for the elements while still letting everyone know you think Tony Stewart is taking the checkered flag. (Do try to avoid wearing checkered-flag clothing, though. It really doesn't look good on anyone.)

While it may not meet the technical definition of clothing, another item you'll find useful and available in any number of racing themes is the fanny pack. These are great for carrying everything from sunscreen and a cell phone to your camera and Sharpie for autograph opportunities. If you don't like the way the fanny pack looks on your fanny, opt for a small backpack.

No matter what you wear, just remember to dress for comfort. You're going to be out there for a few days. It will be hot. It will rain. You need to be prepared.

Not only does what you wear say something about who you are (and who you support), but it can also mean being comfortable for the next several days.

DRESSING FOR HOT WEATHER

Whether you follow stock cars, dragsters, open wheel, or trucks, a good portion of the racing season is in the summer. And a lot of the races are in the South or the desert. It's hot. Really hot. Dangerously hot. Especially for tailgaters who are camped outside the track for four or five days.

So what's your plan? Wear shorts and a T-shirt? That's not enough.

Here's why: people suffer heat-related illnesses when the body's temperature-control system gets overloaded. Normally, your body will cool itself by sweating. But sometimes sweating isn't enough. When the humidity is high, sweat doesn't evaporate as quickly, which prevents the body from releasing heat. When you add other conditions like advanced age, obesity, sunburn, and alcohol, the problem just gets worse. The result can be heat stroke or other ailments that can damage the brain and other organs. Yep, that will ruin your tailgate party in a hurry.

To prevent that from happening to you or your friends, just follow some simple rules and you'll keep your cool.

1. Drink a lot of fluids. In fact, drink more than your thirst tells you to. And I'm talking water here. Beer and other alcohol just make matters worse. In desert areas, it is especially important to remember to keep drinking fluids since you won't sweat like you usually do (part of that whole "it's a dry heat" thing).
2. Wear lightweight, light-colored, loose-fitting clothing.
3. Wear a wide-brimmed hat to provide shade and keep your head cool.
4. Wear sunscreen. You should be doing this anyway, but it's especially important in very hot, sunny conditions. Be sure to use at least SPF 15 and apply it 30 minutes before you walk outside. Read the directions on the sunscreen to know how often to reapply it.
5. Avoid eating heavy meals. They add heat to your body. Eat light foods and eat smaller portions more often. Watch the weather forecast, and plan your menu accordingly. (At theultimatetailgatechef.com you'll find episodes of The Ultimate Tailgate Chef and recipes for tailgating light.)
6. Stay in the shade as much as you can. A tent over your tailgate is a great help. If you don't have a tent, use an umbrella or spend some time in the car with the air on, if it doesn't create exhaust problems for other tailgaters. Or make a new friend with a nice, big, air-conditioned RV, if you don't have one of your own.

If anyone at your tailgate party exhibits signs of heavy sweating, paleness, weakness, vomiting, dizziness, or fainting, get that person to a cool area immediately, give him cool water, and call for medical help. There are medical teams at all tracks who can help you.

On hot days wear loose-fitting, light-weight clothing and plenty of sunscreen.

What the Heck Is Wicking?

It's the garment's ability to absorb sweat, moving it to the surface of the garment where it can evaporate. Wicking shirts come in short sleeve, long sleeve, crew neck, high neck—basically any style you want. Usually, the label will say if the material wicks.

In the summer, these shirts also help you stay cool.

DRESSING FOR COLD WEATHER

While it's not as much of a problem for race fans as hot weather, there are races where it gets awfully cold. Often wet and cold. Especially at night.

Dressing properly for cold weather is just as important as dressing for hot weather, of course. It just takes more gear.

The primary cold weather danger is hypothermia, especially among older people whose skin is less sensitive to the cold, which means they don't feel signs of exposure to dangerously cold temperatures like the rest of us do. If anyone at your tailgate party experiences violent shivering, stops shivering, has slow breathing with a slow pulse, and seems confused, take that person to a warm place and call for medical help.

Staying warm in cold weather is all about insulation. Dressing in layers, if done correctly, creates room for air pockets, which lock in body heat and act as insulation, keeping you warm and happy while you're at the track.

A hat is critical to locking in your body heat, too. Worried about your hat hair and how it will affect your flirting? Get over it. Up to 90 percent of your body heat can be lost through the top of your head. Wear the hat and bring a comb.

Now, dressing in layers doesn't just mean anything on top of anything else. It's important to layer properly.

Inner Layer: This layer should be a material that "wicks" moisture from your body to help keep you dry and comfortable.

Middle Layer: The middle layer should trap warm air and hold it in those air pockets I mentioned earlier. Depending on how cold it is outside, you may need more than one middle layer.

Outer Layer: This layer needs to provide protection from wind, rain, snow, and other cold-weather beasts. It is important for the outer layer to be water resistant enough to keep the inner layers dry.

Down and wool are good materials for the middle layers; a number of synthetic materials are now designed just for this purpose, too. And just because you're trying to stay warm doesn't mean all these layers need to be thick. Your clothes still need to give you freedom of movement. Remember, it's the air pockets keeping you warm.

Finally, don't forget your feet. If your feet are wet and cold, your whole body is going to feel wet and cold. Wear insulated socks with your shoes or boots.

Eating

THE GRILL

Now that you have a place to sleep and you're dressed, it's time to turn your attention to the centerpiece of your tailgate party: the grill. Just as you wouldn't build a home without a kitchen, you can't build the ultimate tailgate party without a grill.

Just as you wouldn't build a home without a kitchen, you can't build the ultimate tailgate party without a grill.

Your first decision is a basic one, but an important one. Charcoal or gas? Which is also to ask, flavor or convenience? This isn't as easy a decision as you might think, and it's one that's pitted brother against brother for generations (okay, for a couple of generations, since the first gas grills were unveiled in 1939).

Many tailgaters will tell you food from a charcoal grill has more flavor and just tastes better. And charcoal grills do cook hotter and make it easy to smoke foods. These are good traits, but there is another half to the story. To maintain even, steady heat, you have to keep an eye on the coals, and they are messy. Plus, you have to deal with the ashes—and tossing them on the grass or in the parking

space next to you isn't how you do that. While some tracks have ash bins scattered around the parking lot for you to dump your ashes in, you always need to bring supplies for taking your ashes out of the parking lot and safely disposing of them. You can't always bet on ash bins being nearby.

Another upside to charcoal grills is they're budget friendly. While some of the larger ones with wheels and other attachments can cost a few hundred dollars, a small, basic charcoal grill costs about $50. But before buying, be sure the grill is sturdy and well constructed. You shouldn't be able to easily dent the metal, the legs must be securely attached, and you'll also want to make sure the unit you buy has vents (so you can control your heat). If you smoke foods, look for one with a front-loading, hinged grill gate.

Many tailgaters will tell you food from a charcoal grill has more flavor and just tastes better.

Setting up at your tailgate party may also play a part in your decision. Charcoal grills take some time and nurturing to get from cold to ready-to-cook. The coals have to heat up, and you have to keep stoking them to keep the fire alive and the heat even. You'll also need a couple bags of coals to make it through the weekend.

Gas grills, on the other hand, take next-to-no setup and start with the push of a button. A standard propane tank lasts about 20 hours. It's easy to keep your heat consistent, and when you're done, you just turn it off.

You can even buy gas grills that attach to your vehicle, leaving more room inside your vehicle for food and supplies, or people. These grills lock down when you go inside the track, so you don't have to worry about leaving enough time for your grill to cool off before putting it away.

When shopping for a gas grill, look for one that has at least two heat zones for indirect cooking (important when cooking foods like ribs on any grill), a built-in temperature gauge, and an easy-to-clean drip pan. Of course, look for sturdy construction and a good warranty, too.

Gas grills take next-to-no setup and start with the push of a button.

MUST-HAVE GRILLING TOOLS

I know what you're thinking: Geez, I grill all the time; I know what I need.

I'm sure you do grill a lot, but at your tailgate party, you don't have your kitchen cabinet on the other side of the door to get the tools you forgot to take outside. And you will forget stuff. Don't believe me? Just ask your wife or buddies. They'll remind you of all those times you did.

So get a duffle bag and put all of these items in it; then all you have to

Space Saver

To save some space in your cooler and have cold water, fill up empty milk jugs or similar containers with water, freeze them, and then use them in your cooler as "ice." When they melt, you won't have a mess and you will have cold water to drink.

do is grab the bag on the way out the door—after washing and cleaning everything from your last tailgate party, of course. (You'll find a complete checklist on page 53.)

First on the list is tongs. These will keep you from using your hands to flip food on the grill. That's a good thing. Get standard-sized tongs; the short ones take up less space but using them means your hands will be directly over the heat. Not a good thing.

Alongside your tongs, you should have spatulas (take at least two), spoons (one of them slotted), a couple of forks, a basting brush, and an instant-read thermometer. That last item is important and could save your life—or at least spare you the embarrassment of giving your guests salmonella poisoning.

Knives are also important. They should be sharp and they should be used only by the cook. Don't use the same knives for food prep and bar prep; that opens the door to cross-contamination. And be sure to have two cutting boards. One you'll use for your meat and the other for vegetables and other items. It's that cross-contamination thing again.

Also add to your bag a couple of pots and pans, even if you don't have a side burner. You wouldn't think of cooking at home without them, so why wouldn't you take them to the parking lot? It may be a grill rather than a stove, but it's all just heat and you'll expand your menus significantly by bringing these along.

Toss these few final items into your cooking bag; they may not traditionally be classified as cooking tools, but you need them. Take an apron (you can find an entire line of driver-styled aprons at coolaprons.com/auto), a couple of hot pads, towels (you can't have too many), and a chef's hat. Okay, you may not need the hat, but you'll sure look good.

ETIQUETTE TIP

#5

Always be aware of which way the wind is blowing your smoke—whether from your grill or a cigarette or cigar. Don't let it bother other tailgaters.

GRILLING EXTRAS TO IMPRESS YOUR FRIENDS

If you want to take your tailgating kitchen up a notch or two, several add-ons will allow you to do more and impress your friends. And I know you want to impress your friends.

First up, the side burner. Some grills have one already, but you can also get it as an optional feature for gas grills (sorry, char-coalers). The side burner offers you the ability to cook with a pot or pan just like you do on the stovetop at home. This means more menu options and more space on your grill for other foods. This is probably the single most useful addition to the basic gas grill.

Skewers and kebab racks come in a close second in the useful category. As any tailgate chef knows, just getting a kebab on and off the grill in one piece can be a challenge. Not any more. Good skewers keep the food in place, and even better, kebab racks let you lift and flip the kebabs without the fear of adding ash to your list of ingredients.

If you want to expand your options and also provide menu items for the more health-conscious in your group, then head to the store and buy a steamer. This will allow you to make a variety of vegetable dishes, seafood, couscous—even desserts (I've seen a steamed cranberry pudding recipe somewhere).

Want to add a pot roast or lamb shank to your tailgate menus? Then just add a Dutch oven to your arsenal. You can cook everything from vegetables to corn-bread to cobbler in this versatile vessel.

A simple add-on is the warming rack. Once you hit a certain price point with gas grills, these usually come standard, but you can also get them as accessories for gas and charcoal grills. We all know how hard it is for your meal to be ready all at once—or for all your friends to be ready all at once—so these little gems come in handy and keep everyone from talking about how your tailgate party was the one with the cold brats.

Now, on the impressive scale, there's one more item that sits near the top: the rotisserie. But in a sense, this means two items since other than a crank-style version or two (and trust me, you don't want to be cranking your chicken for an

Bring pots and pans to expand your menu options, even if you don't have a side burner. Your grill can act as a cooktop, too.

A portable generator can be used to power things like a rotisserie, TV, stereo system, party lights, blender, and more.

hour), these take electricity to work. That means you'll also need to get a portable generator or other power source.

What would you use a rotisserie for? Well, just about anything. You can cook most any meat on a spit, although poultry and lamb are two favorites.

What else would you use a generator for? Well, how about a TV? Or stereo system? Maybe those little chile party lights? A blender would be good. Power can do a lot for a tailgate party. A small generator will be able to handle almost any tailgate need, so you don't have to lug around a unit on wheels to cook Five Spice Duck (talk about impressing friends). Newer generators are pretty quiet, too, so don't worry about yours drowning out the sound on the 42-inch plasma TV hanging from your tent.

THE TAILGATE BAR

Your tailgate bar can be as simple as a cooler with ice and soft drinks or as complex as a setup to rival the Irish pub down the street. The only thing for sure is you're going to need one.

The first step in figuring out your tailgate bar is to think about who is going to be tailgating with you. What do they like? What do they demand? Are there any brand snobs? Or is the only word they care about on the label "beer"? Once you've answered those questions, you'll know whether you need to bring only can coolers— or wine glasses, a blender, garnishes, and a bar caddie. More on those in a bit.

No matter how elaborate your bar is, you need to make sure you have three things: a table (you need a flat surface other than the buffet or the ground), coolers (dedicated for the bar), and ice (lots, and lots, and lots of ice).

Make sure the tables are big enough to hold your bar items and provide enough room to make and pour your drinks. The table legs should have a locking mechanism—asphalt doesn't add to the flavor of a martini, trust me.

As for coolers, get the biggest ones you can easily transport. Coolers are like closets; no matter how big they are, you'll fill them up. Be sure to fill them with ice—lots of ice. You really can't bring too much, and if you run out,

The Quantum Theory

Okay, I'll help you with the Quantum Theory. Pour ¾ ounces rum, ½ ounce Strega herbal liqueur, and ¼ ounce Grand Marnier into a tall glass (a Collins glass is best). Then add 2 ounces pineapple juice and fill the rest of the glass with sweet and sour mix. (If you're not using a Collins-style glass, fill your glass with the sweet and sour mix to taste.)

If your friends try to embarrass you and ask about the other quantum theory, just tell them it's a modern physical theory concerned with the emission and absorption of energy by matter and with the motion of material particles. That'll shut them up.

you can't get more, unless you've made very good friends with the folks in the parking spot next to you.

When tending your tailgate bar, serve responsibly. Many of your guests may be driving home once the race is over, and you want to make sure they make it there.

Tailgating Setups

There's more to a tailgating setup than just parking, setting up your table and chairs, and firing up the grill. A good tailgate setup has flow, and how well it flows determines how much fun you have during your time outside the track.

Think of your tailgate area as you would your home. After all, it is your home for a few days. You don't put the stovetop in your den at home—why would you in the parking lot? No matter how big a setup you have, or how many people you're hosting, there are a few basic points to a good tailgate setup.

THE WORK TRIANGLE

The first point on your triangle is the grill. Be sure to place it away from the rest of your setup. This way you won't crowd the cook or suffocate your guests with smoke. Also, be careful not to place your grill near or under a tent; that could turn out really bad.

The second point of your triangle is the cook's prep table. This area should be near the grill and have its own coolers, cutting board, knives, and trash can—for both convenience and food safety.

The buffet serving table is the final point on the work triangle. It should be set up where people can get to it easily and provide enough space for your guests to put down their drinks and plates when serving themselves.

If you set up your work triangle well, the rest of your tailgate party will fall into place nicely and everyone will have fun.

If you set up your work triangle well, the rest of your tailgate party will fall into place nicely and everyone will have fun.

THE BAR

I've already talked about the bar in detail (see page 30), but it is important to remember to give it its own table, trash can, cooler, and supplies. And be sure not to set it up too close to the buffet serving table—crowding people eager for a drink can cause some mishaps.

CONVERSATION AREA

In the middle of it all is your conversation area. This is where you'll set up chairs, position your stereo and television, and place other items you and your guests will use to pass the time. Be sure to station your generator away from this area so you don't have to talk over it.

Now, with the basics in place, how you finish off your tailgate setup is based on what type of tailgater you are. I've seen several types of tailgaters at tracks across the country, and most of them fall into one of five categories.

1. THE CAMPER

These tailgaters are easily spotted by the added amenities they bring to the track. Many are in RVs outfitted with everything from satellite TV to complete kitchens and entertainment centers, plus "weed-to-weed" carpeting on the ground around their campsite.

Others have family tents with generators providing heat or air conditioning and all the other comforts of home. Some even bring furniture to give it a homey feel.

Either way, these folks are settled in and could camp here for a couple of weeks in comfort and love every minute of it. You'll often find campers riding around the tailgate lots on their bicycles, ATVs, or golf carts.

2. THE LOUNGER

It's all about rest and relaxation for these tailgaters. They may have brought along many of the tools of the camper, but you can tell the difference when you see them rocking in their hammock or kicked back with their feet up, letting the time pass by until it's cocktail hour or the race starts.

It's all about rest and relaxation for the Lounger.

The Ultimate Tailgater's Racing Guide

Some of the added amenities Loungers bring along include electric fans to place outside by their chairs and personal music players with earphones.

3. THE GAMER

No, I'm not talking about video gamers (although you find a lot of those in tailgate neighborhoods, too). I'm talking about the tailgaters for whom the week at the track is all about competition. Sure, the drivers are competing, but it's their own competitions that make the weekend fun.

From Hillbilly Golf, to poker, to who cooks the best burger, these fans fill the day with games and contests. Even the race is opportunity for more competition (see pages 44–46 to learn how to play some games based on what happens on the track).

4. THE CHEF

It's all about the food for these tailgaters. Eating isn't just something you need to do—it's the reason to tailgate.

Don't be surprised to see these tailgaters working with a food processor, blender, or rotisserie. Their tailgate setups often feature multiple grills, all the tools of a home kitchen, and menus

The Gamer fills the day with competition both on and off the track.

The Tailgate Chef prepares full menus, often with themes.

that offer everything from grilled Caesar salad to lobster, ribs, and more. These Tailgate Chefs prepare full menus, often with themes.

5. THE MERCHANT

Handicrafts are often on display outside RVs and tents in racing tailgate neighborhoods. Sometimes they're for sale.

Merchant tailgaters are a relatively small group—after all, many tracks prohibit the selling of any item without a permit—but here and there, you'll find folks selling handmade souvenirs or pieces of artwork. Some enterprising Merchants also sell items you may have forgotten at home.

At some tracks handicrafts are on display or for sale outside RVs and tents in racing tailgate neighborhoods.

Themes and Games

Themes

How do you keep each day of tailgating from being just like yesterday? After all, you're spending a few days in the same spot, with the same neighbors, sometimes eating the same food. (The recipes starting on page 55 will keep you from falling into that last trap.)

The answer is to turn your tailgate party into a theme party for a day. It takes some planning, but I promise you, if you're the tailgater organizing the Oktoberfest, you'll have fun and the rest of the parking lot will be begging you to come back next year.

Since the race schedule lasts pretty much all year, you have several opportunities to theme up your tailgate. Throwing a themed party in the parking lot is like throwing it at your house; the difference is you can't simply run to Target to pick up stuff you forgot. So make sure you have a complete checklist and you take everything you need.

When planning your themed tailgate, think in terms of creating a scene. String up specialty lights, put together a music playlist that fits the theme, dress up in costumes, have contests, and award prizes to the winner.

To spark some ideas, here is a list of common, and not-so-common, holidays and events that can make great tailgate theme parties.

ETIQUETTE TIP

#6

Don't play your music or television loud enough to disturb others.

JANUARY
New Year's Day
MLK Day
American Music Month
National Snack Food Month

FEBRUARY
Groundhog Day
Presidents' Day
Valentine's Day
Fat Tuesday/Mardi Gras
National Soup Month

MARCH
St. Patrick's Day
National Peanut Month
National Frozen Foods Month
National Pig Day (1st)
Albert Einstein's Birthday (14th)

APRIL
National Humor Month
National Guitar Month
Peach Cobbler Day (13th)
Jelly Bean Day (22nd)

MAY
Mother's Day
Memorial Day
Correct Posture Month
International Tuba Day (1st)
Cinco de Mayo

JUNE
Flag Day
Father's Day
National Yo-yo Day (10th)
Fly a Kite Day (15th)
World Juggling Day (18th)

JULY
Independence Day
American Beer Month
National Hot Dog Month
National Ice Cream Month

AUGUST
National Watermelon Day (3rd)
National Champagne Day (4th)
International Left-Handers Day (13th)
Kiss and Make Up Day (25th)

SEPTEMBER
Labor Day
National Tailgating Month
Be Late for Something Day (5th)
National Play-Doh Day (16th)
Ask a Stupid Question Day (30th)

OCTOBER
Columbus Day
National Seafood Month
National Sarcastic Month
National Popcorn Poppin' Month
Halloween

NOVEMBER
Election Day
Thanksgiving
Mickey Mouse's Birthday
(18th)
World Hello Day (21st)

DECEMBER
Hanukkah
Christmas
Kwanzaa

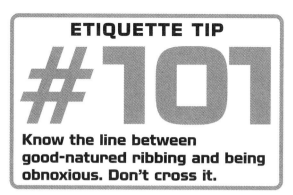

ETIQUETTE TIP

#101

Know the line between good-natured ribbing and being obnoxious. Don't cross it.

In addition to these, you can also throw theme parties based on someone's birthday or a racing team or a driver. That last one could create some spirited conversation—especially after a few drinks—so make sure you have a plan to help keep the peace, if needed.

Games

One thing is for certain when tailgating at a race: you have lots of time on your hands. That's why, in addition to plenty of food and drink, you find a lot of games in racing tailgate neighborhoods.

Take a walk around and you'll see people playing board games, video games, card games, and some games I think they just made up themselves. Who cares? It's fun.

Regardless of which game you play, just two basics make it a good tailgating game. First, be sure it can be played by any number of people. Tailgating is a community activity, and you want to be able to play with your friends; plus games are a great way to make new friends or maybe meet someone who becomes more than a friend—but I'll leave that for a Dr. Phil book.

Second, the game should be easy to understand, no matter how well someone knows racing. It's also good to have some games that require no racing knowledge. After all, tailgating is for everyone.

Rocket Racing League

Okay, I'm not kidding about this.

The guy who created the X-Prize (the $10 million contest to build and fly the first private rocket into space that SpaceShipOne won in 2004) has joined with some traditional race team owners to create the Rocket Racing League, or the RRL. Imagine NASCAR and an air show blended together.

The X-Racers (which is what they call the racing rocket planes) will compete on a 3-dimensional track in the sky. It's about 2 miles long, 1 mile wide, and 5,000 feet high, situated perpendicularly from spectators. X-Racers will take off side-by-side and staggered, and each pilot will fly the course's

straightaways, vertical ascents, and deep banks within his own "tunnel" of space just a few hundred feet from each other. And, yep, they'll come down for pit stops.

Since the track is above them, fans will watch the X-Racers from the grandstands by following 20-foot rocket plumes and colored smoke trails. They can also watch on big-screen TVs and on hand-help GPS devices.

The RRL is being modeled on NASCAR, so expect tailgating areas, merchandise, and everything else that goes along with a land-based race day. Races will be held around the country with the semifinals at the Reno Air Show in September and the finals at the X-PRIZE Cup in New Mexico in October each year.

The creators are working with the FAA on safety issues, but it sure does give another meaning to drafting.

To learn more about the RRL and to find out if there's a race near you, visit rocketracingleague.com.

To get you started, here are a few games and proposition pools you can use to liven up your tailgate party. Some require skill, others just dumb luck, but either way you'll have fun and meet people.

HILLBILLY GOLF

Hillbilly Golf is a good game for large tailgate parties or for battling teams of other tailgaters in your neighborhood. (In different regions this game goes by other names, too. So if you think this sounds a lot like Ladder Golf, for example, it's the same game. It's just that in racing tailgate lots, I hear most people call it Hillbilly Golf, so I'm going with that.)

The object is to score more points wrapping your bolas around the steps of the ladder than your opponent does. Your bola is not next to your pancreas; it's two golf balls attached by a rope that you toss at the ladder.

You can find everything you need to play Hillbilly Golf at a number of stores and Web sites, including laddergolf.com.

The setup: If you have one ladder, mark a toss line 15 feet from it. That's

Hillbilly Golf is a good game for large tailgate parties or for battling teams of other tailgaters in your neighborhood.

where you'll stand to toss your bola. If you have two ladders, set them up 15 feet from each other and divide your teams on either end.

How to play: You play Hillbilly Golf in rounds. One round is when both players throw all three of their bolas toward the ladder. (If playing with teams, a member of each team tosses a round, thus alternating rounds between team members.) You can throw your bola any way you like, and it's legal for it to bounce off the ground and to knock other players' bolas off the ladder. Any bolas knocked off the ladder do not earn points.

Games are played until a player or team scores exactly 21 points. To win, a player must be the only one to score exactly 21 points after the completion of a round. If you go over 21, that round doesn't count.

If there's a tie, the tied players (or teams) toss as many overtime rounds as needed for one of them to complete a round two points ahead, which gives that player (or team) the win.

Scoring: Scoring is determined by the bolas that are still hanging from the steps at the end of the round. Points are determined by which step your bola is wrapped around. The top step is worth 3 points, the middle step is worth 2 points, and the bottom step earns 1 point. You can also include in your rules a bonus point for players who hang all three bolas from the same step or hang a bola on each of the three steps in the same round.

WASHERS

Washers is another good game for groups and teams. It's a game similar to horseshoes, but you toss washers (as in nuts and bolts, not as in washers and dryers—although that would be impressive) into a hole cut from a wooden box.

The setup: The boxes are placed at least 20 feet apart on as level a surface as you can find. (You decide how far apart to place them, based on how much of a challenge you're up for.)

How to play: One player stands behind the front edge of one box and tosses each of his three washers toward the other box. The next player then does the same. You can throw the washers any way you like, although veterans will tell you to go with the underhanded toss. The highest score wins the round.

It's good to have some games that require no racing knowledge. After all, tailgating is for everyone.

Scoring: If your washer lands on the box, you score 1 point; if it goes in the hole, you earn 3 points. The player with the highest score wins the round, and the first player or team to reach 21 wins the game. There is one more scoring rule: if both players' washers land on the box or in the hole, they cancel each other out and no one gets a point.

You can buy washers and boxes on a number of Web sites, or you can build your own box and use washers from the hardware store (be sure to get the big, oversized washers, not the ones you use on regular screws). One enthusiast who goes by the screen name "BenRod" has a step-by-step photo guide for building a box on flickr.com—search for "How to Build a Game of Washers."

There're also popular versions of this game called Corn Hole and Bean Bag Toss that use bean bags instead of washers—otherwise, the rules are the same. Many of the Web sites that sell washer game sets also carry these versions of the game. Baggo.com sells a version that folds into a carrying case, although you'll have to add your own racing logos; the company concentrates on the football market.

PROPOSITION POOLS

The basic premise of these pools is that people make predictions before the race and what happens on the track determines the winner. It helps if you do your homework on who's who and who's racing well, but since even the best driver can hit the wall on turn four, even a racing novice can win.

NASCAR KENO

Number of players: 2–10

To win: Match your number most often with the last digit of the lap leader for each segment.

This is a simple game to play, and you can devise a number of variations—be creative! It is also a game that will have participants cheering for and against their favorite drivers at certain points of the race.

Before the race, each player draws a number between 0 and 9 from a hat. The participant gets 1 point for each 10-lap segment in which his or her number matches the last digit of the lap leader's car number. The checkered flag is the final segment, and the player with the most points wins. (Obviously, the game's more fun with 10 players than with 2, since with fewer players there's a chance no one will win.)

THE CHECKERED FLAG PROPOSITION POOL

Number of players: 2+

To win: Earn the most points by correctly predicting the events of the race.

Score 2 points for each correct prediction in questions 1–7 and get points for accuracy in question 8; the person with the most points wins.

Pole sitter leads at the end of Lap 1 ____Yes ____No

Leader with 10 laps to go wins race ____Yes ____No

Margin of victory is less than 1 second ____Yes ____No

Winning driver leads the most laps ____Yes ____No

Cautions outnumber lap leaders ____Yes ____No

Pole sitter finishes in the top 5 ____Yes ____No

The race ends under a caution flag ____Yes ____No

Select three drivers (in any order) and score 5 points if the race winner is among your selected drivers, 3 points if the second place finisher is one of your three, and 1 point if the third place finisher is in your list.

Drivers:

1

_____ .

2

_____ .

3

_____ .

Tie breaker:
Finishing position of the pole sitter _____

SCAVENGER HUNTS

This is the same game you played as a kid, except instead of knocking on your neighbor's door asking for a roll of toilet paper, you're wandering up to someone's RV asking to take a picture of them in their Dale Jr. halter top.

To play, simply select your items and prepare item lists for your teams. It's best to have teams of two or three so that it's easier to canvass the parking lots and you don't have a gaggle of people asking the same tailgaters for the same things. You don't make as many new friends that way.

When all your teams have gathered, hand out the item lists, tell everyone how much time they have (give yourselves at least an hour or so since you know you'll want to stop and talk with people—which is what tailgating is all about), remind them to take their digital cameras, and set them loose. The first team that gets back to the tailgate with a completed list is the winner.

I've put together the list below to get you started on some items to search for. Don't stick to it. Add your own items to the list, and change it up race-to-race to keep the games fresh and fun and appropriate for the type of race you're attending. Your NASCAR list will be different from your IHRA list. And don't overload the list, either. About a dozen items per game works well.

Collect or take digital pictures of the items listed:

- [ ] #20 hitch cover
- [ ] #24 coffee mug
- [ ] #55 coffee mug
- [ ] #3 earrings
- [ ] #2 hat
- [ ] #16 hitch cover
- [ ] #8 coffee mug
- [ ] #9 hat
- [ ] Adult with face painted
- [ ] Autographed picture of driver
- [ ] Beer can with NASCAR driver/team on it
- [ ] Black cowboy hat
- [ ] Cake shaped as speedway
- [ ] Celebrity
- [ ] Checkered flag
- [ ] Checkered flag napkins
- [ ] Checkered flag pattern sneakers
- [ ] Checkered flag shirt
- [ ] Checkered flag tablecloth
- [ ] Clothing item with multiple driver autographs
- [ ] Custom-painted gas grill
- [ ] Driver hat autographed by the driver
- [ ] Driver tattoo (real one, not temporary)
- [ ] Elvis impersonator
- [ ] Former driver

- [ ] License plate that says "The King"
- [ ] Map of track
- [ ] NASCAR tailgate table
- [ ] Person with a car number painted on his chest
- [ ] Picture of Dale and Dale Jr. together
- [ ] Picture of driver in golf cart
- [ ] Picture of Lil' E with no baseball hat on
- [ ] Professional athlete
- [ ] Race car–shaped grill
- [ ] Racing gear with clock attached
- [ ] Remote control car
- [ ] Someone from a foreign country (they must have a passport)
- [ ] Toddler in cool-looking shades
- [ ] Toddler with face painted

Planning Guide/Checklists

When you prepare to go on vacation, you take some time to map out a plan. You chart your course on maps, you write checklists, you start putting things together weeks before you leave.

I know many tailgaters don't think of a race trip as a vacation because they do it several times a year, but the mechanics are a lot alike. After all, you'll be gone for a few days. But unlike many vacations, you'll often find yourself in a field or parking lot with only what you packed available for food and comfort.

That's what these next few pages are about.

Racing tailgaters have a lot of gear and prerace prep. Here, I've broken everything down into several checklists to help you organize your trip. Many tailgaters write out their checklists, laminate them, and attach them to the top of their storage bins or coolers. Then they use a grease pencil to check off items before each race. It's a handy trick.

Before the Trip

How much you have to do in the weeks running up to your trip is based on how you plan to get there. This checklist will help you with the most important items. If you need a more detailed traveling checklist, you can find one in *The Ultimate Tailgater's Travel Guide* and at theultimatetailgater.com.

- ☐ Reconfirm lodging/camping reservations (best to do this a couple weeks early).
- ☐ Review your destination's tailgating rules and any restrictions.
- ☐ If traveling in a group, divide up who is bringing what (including food).
- ☐ Confirm you have all the maps you'll need.
- ☐ Have your vehicle's oil and fluids checked, tires properly inflated, etc.

☐ Charge your cell phone the night before you leave.

☐ Gas up your vehicle the day before you leave (even if you're just going to the airport).

☐ Make sure you have your driver's license, credit cards, and race tickets (and plane tickets if flying).

☐ If driving an RV, check levels of tanks and pretreat water tanks.

☐ Check road conditions before leaving (fhwa.dot.gov/trafficinfo/).

FOR YOUR VEHICLE

Some of these items are also important when you get to the track (like the first aid kit), but make sure they're easily accessible during your trip.

☐ Blankets

☐ Deicer

☐ First Aid Kit

  ☐ Alcohol swabs/antiseptic wipes

  ☐ Triple antibiotic ointment

  ☐ Hydrocortisone cream

  ☐ Adhesive bandages

  ☐ Sterile gauze pads

  ☐ First-aid tape

  ☐ Scissors (may not be able to take on airplanes)

  ☐ One or two elastic bandages

  ☐ Burn creams (including sunburn creams)

  ☐ Ibuprofen or acetaminophen

  ☐ Aspirin

  ☐ Antacids

  ☐ Tweezers

  ☐ Disposable instant cold pack

  ☐ Thermometer

  ☐ Plastic/latex gloves

☐ Fix-a-Flat (or similar brand)

☐ Flares

- ☐ Jumper cables
- ☐ Map(s)
- ☐ Rags
- ☐ Water
- ☐ Wiper fluid

FOR YOUR TAILGATE SITE

Depending on your type of shelter, some of these may not apply, but remember to take everything you just might need, since getting it later will be tough. (I didn't put your tent or RV on the list—surely you remembered that yourself.)

- ☐ Air mattress
- ☐ Air pump
- ☐ Ant spray
- ☐ Antibacterial soap
- ☐ Batteries
- ☐ Broom
- ☐ Bungee cords
- ☐ Camp stool
- ☐ Canopy
- ☐ Cards
- ☐ Citronella candles
- ☐ Cloth towels
- ☐ Clothesline
- ☐ Clothespins
- ☐ Collapsible table and chairs
- ☐ Decorations
- ☐ Different-sized/thickness pieces of boards (for leveling)
- ☐ Doormat
- ☐ Duct tape
- ☐ Extension cords
- ☐ Firewood

- [ ] Flashlight
- [ ] Games
- [ ] Groundsheet
- [ ] Hair dryer
- [ ] Insect repellent
- [ ] Lantern (propane)
- [ ] Linens
- [ ] Matches
- [ ] Moist towelettes
- [ ] Paper towels
- [ ] Pillows
- [ ] Port-a-potty (check regulations first)
- [ ] Potty chemicals
- [ ] Propane
- [ ] Reading lantern
- [ ] Reading materials
- [ ] Rope
- [ ] Shower
- [ ] Shower stall
- [ ] Sleeping bags
- [ ] Sleeping pads
- [ ] Stakes (plastic/metal)
- [ ] Sunglasses
- [ ] Sunscreen
- [ ] Tarps
- [ ] Tie straps
- [ ] Toilet paper
- [ ] Toiletries
- [ ] Trash bags
- [ ] Trash cans
- [ ] Umbrella

FOR COOKING

Food is the centerpiece of your tailgate party, and no one wants to eat a burger made on the asphalt because someone forgot to bring a plate. Be sure to double check your recipe list to make sure you pack all of your ingredients.

- [ ] Aluminum foil
- [ ] Apron
- [ ] Ash container
- [ ] Basting brush
- [ ] Bottle opener
- [ ] Can opener
- [ ] Charcoal
- [ ] Cleaning supplies
- [ ] Cloth towels
- [ ] Coffee
- [ ] Coffee pot
- [ ] Coolers
- [ ] Corkscrew
- [ ] Cutting boards (two or more)
- [ ] Dishwashing liquid
- [ ] Food
- [ ] Food storage containers
- [ ] Grill/stovetop/burner
- [ ] Ice (lots and lots of it)
- [ ] Kitchen knives
- [ ] Latex gloves
- [ ] Measuring cups/spoons
- [ ] Paper towels
- [ ] Plates/bowls/cups
- [ ] Potholder
- [ ] Pots and pans
- [ ] Serving dishes
- [ ] Serving spoons/forks

- ☐ Spatulas (two or more)
- ☐ Spices
- ☐ Thermometer (instant-read type)
- ☐ Tongs (two or more)
- ☐ Towels
- ☐ Trash bags
- ☐ Trash cans
- ☐ Zip-top bags

For the Race

Check the Track Guides beginning on page 111 to see what you can take into the stands at Nextel Cup races. But rules do change, so before you leave for any race, be sure to visit the track's Web site.

- ☐ Batteries
- ☐ Binoculars
- ☐ Blanket
- ☐ Camera
- ☐ Ear plugs
- ☐ Eye drops
- ☐ Face paint
- ☐ Gum
- ☐ Insulated drink holders
- ☐ Moist towelettes
- ☐ Radio/CD player
- ☐ Scanners
- ☐ Seat cushions
- ☐ Sun/rain gear
- ☐ Sunglasses
- ☐ Sunscreen
- ☐ TV (portable)
- ☐ Umbrella
- ☐ Water

Tailgating Recipes

The great thing about tailgating at races is you have time to cook. While your friends at football games are trying to parboil ribs and figure out how to cook a spread inside of two hours, you have all day to slow-cook your ribs to perfection. You also get to try out several recipes since you're camped out for a few days.

An awful lot of readers of *American Profile* magazine have spent time tailgating across the country. On the next several pages, you'll find some of their best recipes. And if you come to any of our Party in the Pits tailgating events around the country, stop by for my take on a few of these great recipes. (Click on the Party in the Pits link at theultimatetailgater.com to learn more. If you have some recipes of your own to share, click on "Recipes," and send them to me. You just might end up in a book!)

A couple of notes about tailgate cooking and these recipes. First, I've included several recipes you can make at home before you leave for the race (look for the), so the most you'll have to do at the track is heat them up. Of course, if you're tailgating in an RV with a kitchen, you'll have plenty of time to make these dishes at the track.

That leads to my second point. Several dishes, like casseroles, call for heating an oven to a certain temperature. If you are cooking on a grill, you can use it as an oven. Just heat your grill to the same temperature (you can use an ordinary oven thermometer if your grill doesn't have one built in) and place the dish on the grill. Close the lid and you have a tailgate oven. You'll need to keep your eye on the grill to make sure the temperature stays consistent, but it will cook the dish just like an oven will. Just be sure to use aluminum baking dishes rather than glass or ceramic. They work better and are easier to clean.

Earlier, in the section on must-have grilling tools, I said to be sure to toss some pots and pans in your tailgate bag, even if you don't have a side burner on your grill, since it will expand your menus significantly. You'll find some of those menu expanders on the next several pages. Just put those pans on your grill and sauté and fry like you would at home. After all, it's all heat and that's what cooks the food, of course.

If you want even more recipes for your tailgate party, you'll find them, along with food and cooking videos and podcasts, at theultimatetailgatechef.com.

Food

Breakfast

Appetizers

Breads, Salads, Soups, Sides

Blueberry Coffee Cake

Coffee Cake:

½ cup solid vegetable shortening

1 cup sugar

2 eggs

1 teaspoon vanilla extract

2 ¼ cups all-purpose flour

1 tablespoon baking powder

⅔ cup milk

2 cups fresh or frozen blueberries

Topping:

⅔ cup sugar

⅔ cup all-purpose flour

½ cup butter

¼ teaspoon almond extract

Preheat the oven to 350°.

Lightly grease and flour two 9-inch-round baking pans. In a large mixing bowl, beat the shortening and sugar together until light and fluffy. Add the eggs and vanilla. Beat well. In a separate bowl, stir together the flour and baking powder. Add this alternately with the milk to the shortening mixture. When smooth, divide the batter into the two baking pans. Spoon 1 cup blueberries over the batter in each pan.

For the topping, combine the sugar, flour, butter, and almond extract until crumbly. Sprinkle the mixture over the blueberries. Bake for about 35 minutes, or until the center is done.

Makes 20 to 30 slices.

FOOD SAFETY TIP

#19

Always store perishable foods at 40 degrees Fahrenheit or less to prevent illness.

Breakfast Casserole

6 slices white bread

1 pound sausage

1 teaspoon dry mustard

5 eggs

2 cups milk

1 teaspoon Worcestershire sauce

¼ teaspoon salt

¼ teaspoon pepper

2 cups grated Swiss cheese

Preheat the oven to 350°.

Grease a lasagna pan large enough to hold the slices of bread in one layer. Brown the sausage in a skillet and mix it with the dry mustard. In a large bowl, beat the eggs and milk together with the Worcestershire sauce, salt, and pepper. Layer the ingredients in the pan, putting the bread first, then the sausage, then the grated cheese. Finally pour the egg mixture over all. Refrigerate overnight. Bake for 30 to 45 minutes.

Makes 6 servings.

Breakfast Pizza

1 (8-ounce) can refrigerated crescent rolls

6 eggs, beaten

½ pound bacon, cooked and crumbled

1 ½ cups shredded Cheddar cheese

1 (4-ounce) can sliced mushrooms, drained

Preheat the grill to medium-high heat (or the oven to 375º). Unroll the dough and press it into an even layer, covering the bottom of a lightly greased, 12-inch pizza pan. Combine the eggs, bacon, cheese, and mushrooms; pour the mixture evenly over the dough. Cook 15 to 20 minutes, or until the eggs are firm and the crust is golden.

Makes 3 to 6 servings.

Caramel-Pecan French Toast

½ cup butter, melted

½ cup maple syrup

1 teaspoon vanilla extract

1 loaf French bread, cut into 1-inch-thick slices

3 eggs, beaten

⅔ cup whole milk

¼ teaspoon salt

¼ teaspoon pepper

¾ cup chopped pecans

Combine the butter, syrup, and vanilla in a small bowl. Pour the mixture into a 13 x 9-inch baking dish. Place the bread in a single layer over the syrup mixture. Whisk together the eggs, milk, salt, and pepper, and pour the egg mix over the bread. Sprinkle the pecans on top. Cover with plastic wrap, and refrigerate for 8 to 10 hours or overnight.

Preheat the oven to 350º. Uncover the dish and bake for 1 hour.

Makes 6 servings.

Spiced Apple Pancakes

1 cup all-purpose flour

2 tablespoons sugar

2 teaspoons baking powder

½ teaspoon cinnamon

¼ teaspoon ground ginger

¼ teaspoon allspice

1 egg

¾ cup milk

2 tablespoons molasses

1 tablespoon vegetable oil

2 apples, peeled and diced

Combine the flour, sugar, baking powder, cinnamon, ginger, and allspice in a medium-size bowl. In a small bowl, beat the egg, and combine it with the milk, molasses, and oil until well blended. Pour the wet mixture into the dry mixture, and stir until just evenly blended. Stir in the apples. Pour ¼ cup batter onto a hot, lightly greased griddle. Cook 2 to 3 minutes on each side, making certain the center is cooked through. Repeat with the remaining batter.

Makes 2 to 4 servings.

Chicken Fingers

2 ½ pounds boneless, skinless chicken

1 cup milk

1 egg, beaten

1 cup all-purpose flour

Salt and pepper

1 cup cooking oil

1 stick butter

¼ cup Louisiana hot sauce (or more to taste)

FOOD SAFETY TIP

#76

Never defrost foods outside at a tailgate party.

Preheat the oven to 350°.

Cut the chicken into 2- to 3-inch slices. Combine the milk with the beaten egg, and dip the chicken slices in the egg/milk mixture. Then mix the flour with salt and pepper to taste, and coat the chicken with the flour mixture. Heat the oil in a large frying pan, and brown the chicken fingers. Melt the butter in a large baking dish. Stir in the hot sauce, place the browned chicken fingers in the dish, cover with aluminum foil, and bake for 30 minutes.

Makes 4 to 6 servings.

Creole Corn Salsa

1 (15-ounce) can whole kernel corn, drained
1 cup drained chopped tomatoes
½ cup chopped onion
½ teaspoon minced garlic
¼ cup chopped green bell pepper
2 tablespoons olive oil
2 tablespoons lime juice
2 tablespoons vinegar
1 teaspoon Creole seasoning
Tortilla chips for serving

In a large bowl, mix the corn, tomatoes, onion, garlic, and green pepper. In a separate small bowl, whisk together the olive oil, lime juice, vinegar, and Creole seasoning. Pour the olive oil mixture over the vegetables, and stir well. Cover and refrigerate for at least 1 to 2 hours before serving. Serve with tortilla chips.

Makes 8 to 10 servings.

Fiesta Bean and Beef Dip

1 pound ground beef

1 medium onion, chopped

1 package taco seasoning

1 (10-ounce) can Rotel tomatoes and green chiles

1 (15-ounce) can pinto beans, mashed

1 pound Velveeta cheese, cut into cubes

Tortilla chips for serving

Brown the meat with the onion. Drain off the grease. Add the taco seasoning and amount of water suggested on the taco packet. Add the tomatoes and chiles, beans, and cheese. Heat thoroughly. Serve immediately with tortilla chips.

Makes 24 to 30 servings.

Maryland Crab Cakes

1 egg

½ cup mayonnaise

1 tablespoon chopped parsley

1 teaspoon dry mustard

½ teaspoon Old Bay seasoning

½ teaspoon baking powder

1 teaspoon Worcestershire sauce

Pinch of white pepper

1 slice white bread without crust, crumbed

1 pound back fin crabmeat

1 tablespoon cooking oil or butter

Combine the egg, mayonnaise, parsley, dry mustard, Old Bay, baking powder, Worcestershire sauce, and white pepper in a bowl and mix well. Fold in the bread crumbs and crabmeat gently, and form into cakes. Sauté in the oil or butter.

Makes 4 servings.

Party Cheese Ball

8 ounces grated Cheddar cheese

8 ounces softened cream cheese

½ medium onion, minced

2 tablespoons dried chives, or 3 tablespoons fresh, finely chopped

2 tablespoons mayonnaise

½ cup chopped fresh parsley

1 cup well chopped pecans

Mix together the cheeses, onion, chives, and mayonnaise, and form a ball. Roll the ball in the parsley and pecans until evenly coated. Chill until serving time.

Makes 8 to 10 servings.

Salmon Dip

1 (15-ounce) can salmon

1 (8-ounce) package cream cheese, softened

⅓ small onion, chopped

1 tablespoon lemon juice

½ teaspoon prepared horseradish

¼ teaspoon liquid smoke

Salt

Remove the bones and skin from the salmon. Mix with the cream cheese, onion, lemon juice, horseradish, liquid smoke, and salt to taste. Refrigerate until ready to eat. Serve with crackers.

Makes 8 to 10 servings.

Sausage-Stuffed Mushrooms

1 ½ pounds medium mushrooms (about 30)
½ pound bulk pork sausage
¼ cup chopped onion
½ cup shredded Mozzarella cheese
½ cup shredded pepper Jack cheese
¼ cup seasoned bread crumbs

Preheat the oven to 450°.

Remove the mushroom stems from the mushroom caps, and chop the stems very finely. Set aside the stems. Place the mushroom caps in a shallow baking dish in a single layer.

In a skillet, brown the sausage, and drain it well on paper towels. Reserve a small amount of sausage grease in the pan. Crumble the sausage and set it aside.

In the reserved grease, lightly brown the onion. Add the chopped mushroom stems, and cook until tender. Remove from the heat. Stir in the cheeses, bread crumbs, and sausage, and mix well. Spoon the filling into the mushroom caps. Bake for 15 minutes. Serve hot.

Makes about 30.

Sugared Pecans

1 egg white

1 tablespoon water

1 cup sugar

1 teaspoon salt

1 teaspoon cinnamon

1 pound pecan halves

Preheat the oven to 300°. Beat the egg white with the water until frothy. In a large zip-top plastic bag, combine the sugar, salt, and cinnamon. Dip the pecans in the egg white. Place the coated pecans in the plastic bag containing the sugar mixture, and shake to coat well. Place on a well-greased shallow baking sheet. Bake 40 minutes or until the egg white is dry. Stir every 10 minutes. Cool on waxed paper.

Makes 8 to 10 servings.

Pumpkin Bread

2 eggs

1 ¾ cups sugar

1 cup canned pumpkin

½ teaspoon salt

1 teaspoon cinnamon

1 teaspoon freshly grated nutmeg

½ cup vegetable oil

⅓ cup water

1 teaspoon baking soda

1 ¾ cups all-purpose flour

1 tablespoon vanilla extract

1 cup chopped black walnuts

Preheat the oven to 350°.

Grease and flour two 9 x 5-inch loaf pans. In a large mixing bowl, combine the eggs, sugar, pumpkin, salt, cinnamon, and nutmeg. Stir in the oil, water, baking soda, flour, vanilla, and walnuts until well blended. Divide the batter equally between the pans. Bake for 45 minutes. Reduce the oven temperature to 250°, and continue baking the loaves for an additional 15 minutes, or until a toothpick inserted in the center comes out clean. (This is great served with real whipped cream and a dash of ground nutmeg.)

Makes 2 loaves, 20 to 30 slices.

Banana Bread

1 ¾ cups all-purpose flour
¼ teaspoon salt
1 teaspoon baking soda
1 ½ sticks butter, softened
1 ½ cups sugar
2 eggs
¼ cup buttermilk
1 teaspoon vanilla extract
½ to 1 cup chopped nuts
1 cup well-mashed, overripe bananas

Glaze:
1 cup confectioners' sugar
2 to 3 tablespoons lemon juice

Preheat the oven to 350°.

Grease and flour two 8 ½ by 4 ½-inch loaf pans. Combine the flour, salt, and baking soda. Cream together the butter and sugar until light and fluffy. Add the eggs one at a time, beating well after each addition. Add the flour mixture alternately with the buttermilk. Beat the batter for 2 to 3 minutes. Stir in the vanilla, nuts, and bananas. Spoon into the loaf pans. Bake about 50 minutes, or until a toothpick inserted in the center comes out clean. Cool before adding the glaze.

For the glaze, stir the confectioners' sugar and lemon juice together until smooth. Pour over the cooled loaves.

Makes 2 loaves, 20 to 30 slices.

Cole Slaw and Dressing

Dressing:

¾ cup mayonnaise

3 tablespoons sugar

1 ½ tablespoons white wine vinegar

⅓ cup vegetable oil

⅛ teaspoon garlic powder

⅛ teaspoon onion powder

⅛ teaspoon dry mustard

⅛ teaspoon celery salt

Dash of pepper

1 tablespoon lemon juice

½ cup half-and-half

¼ teaspoon salt or more to taste

FOOD SAFETY TIP

#99

Raw meats and ready-to-eat foods should always be kept in separate coolers and containers.

Cole Slaw:

1 large green cabbage head, finely shredded

Purple cabbage and carrots, finely shredded (optional)

For the dressing, blend together the mayonnaise, sugar, vinegar, and oil. Add the garlic and onion powders, dry mustard, celery salt, pepper, lemon juice, half-and-half, and salt. Stir until smooth. Refrigerate until ready to use.

For the cole slaw, pour the dressing over the green cabbage. Purple cabbage and carrots can be added for color. Toss until the vegetables are well-coated.

Makes 6 to 8 servings.

Roasted Potato Salad

4 cups red potatoes
Vegetable oil or cooking spray
2 hard-cooked eggs, chopped
6 slices bacon, crisply cooked and crumbled
¼ cup finely chopped onion
½ to 1 cup mayonnaise
Salt and pepper

Preheat the oven to 325°.

Scrub the potatoes and cut them into bite-size pieces,
leaving the skins on. Roast the potatoes on a lightly oiled cookie sheet
until tender, about 25 minutes. Allow them to cool. Mix the potatoes with
the eggs, bacon, onion, mayonnaise, and salt and pepper to taste. Chill
thoroughly.

Makes 6 to 8 servings.

Supreme Chicken Salad

2 whole boneless chicken breasts
1 rib celery
1 small onion, quartered
1 cup finely chopped celery
1 ½ to 2 cups mayonnaise
2 tablespoons lemon juice
Salt and pepper
Romaine lettuce

Place the chicken breasts in a saucepan and cover with water. Boil with the celery rib and quartered onion for about 20 minutes until the chicken is done. Set aside to cool. Drain and discard the vegetables. Chop the cooked chicken in a food processor or meat grinder. Combine the chopped celery, mayonnaise, lemon juice, and salt and pepper to taste with the chicken in a medium-size bowl. Add additional seasoning according to taste. Serve chilled on the Romaine lettuce.

Makes 8 to 10 servings.

Fiesta Black Bean Salad

2 cups fresh, canned, or frozen corn

½ purple onion, diced

1 red bell pepper, diced

2 (15-ounce) cans black beans, rinsed and drained

3 teaspoons chili powder

2 tablespoons olive oil

¼ teaspoon garlic powder

⅛ teaspoon salt

2 tablespoons balsamic vinegar

2 tablespoons lemon juice

½ cup minced fresh cilantro

Pepper

Gently toss together the corn, onion, red pepper, and beans. Stir in the chili powder and allow to sit at room temperature. Meanwhile, whisk together the olive oil, garlic powder, salt, vinegar, and lemon juice. Pour over the vegetables. Stir in the cilantro and season with pepper to taste. Chill for 2 hours before serving.

Makes 6 servings.

Cool Fruit Salad

1 pint whipping cream

1 (8-ounce) can crushed pineapple, drained

1 (6-ounce) jar maraschino cherries, drained and halved

2 bananas, chopped

¾ cup small marshmallows

2 tablespoons mayonnaise

1 tablespoon sifted confectioners' sugar

Whip the cream and fold in the fruits and marshmallows. Mix the mayonnaise and confectioners' sugar, and add to the fruit mixture. Freeze in a flat 9 by 10-inch pan. Cut the salad in squares and serve on lettuce leaves.

Makes 4 to 8 servings.

Fall Potato Soup

10 to 12 small new red potatoes,
or 4 to 5 medium-size potatoes

1 carrot, grated

¼ onion, finely chopped

1 rib celery, finely chopped

2 tablespoons butter

1 tablespoon bacon grease

1 teaspoon all-purpose flour

1 (14-ounce) can chicken broth

1 cup milk

Salt and pepper

Cheddar cheese, grated

Green onions, chopped

Steam the potatoes until very tender. Peel and cut into bite-size pieces when cool. Sauté the carrot, onion, and celery in the butter until crisp-tender.

Stir in the bacon grease and flour. Pour in the chicken broth and milk, and stir until smooth. Add the potatoes and salt and pepper; stir until the mixture is lump-free. Heat to the boiling point, but do not boil. To serve, top with grated Cheddar cheese and chopped green onions.

Makes 6 to 10 servings.

ETIQUETTE TIP

#7

Don't participate in food fights. Even if you didn't start it.

Pumpkin Soup

½ *small yellow onion, diced*

6 tablespoons butter

½ *cup all-purpose flour*

4 cups chicken or vegetable broth

1 (15-ounce) can pumpkin

½ *cup apple juice*

Dash of salt and pepper

1 ½ cups heavy cream

Sauté the onion in the butter in a heavy saucepan over medium heat until translucent. Do not allow the onions to burn. Add the flour and continue to cook for about 10 minutes, stirring often. Slowly stir in the broth. Add the pumpkin, apple juice, salt, and pepper. Heat thoroughly. Puree the mixture in a blender, and return the soup to the saucepan. Add the cream and heat to serve.

Makes 8 to 12 servings.

Super Bowl of Chili

Canola or olive oil as needed for sautéing

4 cups chopped onions

2 cups chopped celery

6 garlic cloves, minced

2 pounds lean ground beef (ground chicken or turkey also can be used; for variety when using beef, try mixing in a little ground pork)

3 tablespoons chili powder

1 teaspoon cumin seeds

Salt and pepper

1 (28-ounce) can crushed tomatoes

1 (8-ounce) can tomato sauce

1 (28-ounce) can water

2 (15-ounce) cans kidney beans

2 chicken bouillon cubes

Cayenne pepper (I use about 2 pinches for a mild chili with a little zing.)

Place a small amount of oil (start with a tablespoon or so) in a large Dutch oven. Add the onions, celery, and garlic, and sauté until the vegetables are soft, adding a bit more oil if needed. In a separate frying pan, brown the meat; drain and add the meat to the vegetables. Stir in the chili powder, cumin, and salt and pepper to taste. Then add the tomatoes and tomato sauce. Fill the crushed tomatoes can with water and add the water.

Bring the mixture to a boil, turn it down, and simmer, partly covered, for 1 ½ hours, stirring occasionally to avoid burning. After the first half hour, drain and rinse the beans and add them to the chili. Stir in the bouillon cubes as well. After the second half hour, taste the chili and add more salt and pepper if desired, and more cayenne if you like a bit more spice.

Makes 8 to 10 servings.

Blue Cheese Mashed Red Potatoes

8 to 10 medium red potatoes
5 cloves garlic, halved
2 tablespoons crumbled blue cheese
1 tablespoon mayonnaise
1 tablespoon butter
1 cup milk or cream
Salt and pepper

Wash the potatoes, but do not peel. Boil them for about 20 minutes. Add the garlic cloves, and continue to cook until the potatoes are tender.

Set out the measured amounts of cheese, mayonnaise, butter, and milk and bring these ingredients to room temperature. When the potatoes and garlic are soft enough to mash, remove from the heat and drain. Place in a large bowl, and blend with the cheese, mayonnaise, butter, and milk, adding only ½ cup milk to start. Whip the potatoes until fluffy. Adjust the amount of milk to achieve the desired consistency. Season with salt and pepper to taste.

Makes 4 to 6 servings.

Broccoli Casserole

1 egg, beaten

1 onion, finely chopped

8 ounces fat-free sour cream

1 (10 ½-ounce) can cream of broccoli soup, undiluted

1 (10-ounce) box frozen broccoli pieces, thawed

1 (8-ounce) package corn bread stuffing, divided

16 ounces grated cheese, divided

2 tablespoons butter

Preheat the oven to 350º.

Spray a casserole dish with cooking spray. In a large bowl, mix the egg, onion, sour cream, soup, broccoli, half the corn bread stuffing, and half the cheese. Pour into the casserole dish. Mix the remaining stuffing and cheese and add the butter. Mix well and spread over the top of the casserole. Bake for 30 minutes or until lightly browned.

Makes 12 servings.

Lemon Asparagus

1 ½ pounds fresh asparagus

3 to 5 tablespoons butter

Juice and zest of 1 lemon

¼ cup water

1 teaspoon salt

¼ teaspoon pepper

Break the tough ends off the asparagus. Rinse and remove the scales with a carrot peeler. Heat the butter, lemon juice and zest, and water in a large skillet to boiling. Add the asparagus, salt, and pepper. Cover and simmer for 3 to 5 minutes, or until crisp-tender. Serve immediately.

Makes 6 to 10 servings.

Country-Fried Steaks

4 to 6 large cube steaks
½ cup all-purpose flour
Salt and pepper

½ stick butter
½ package Lipton Onion Soup Mix

Dredge the steaks in the flour, shaking off excess. Add salt and pepper to taste. Melt the butter over medium heat in a large skillet. Brown the steaks well on both sides. Add enough water to cover the steaks completely. Sprinkle the soup mix evenly in the water. Cover and simmer the steaks for 40 minutes.

Makes 4 to 8 servings.

Grilled Chili Flank Steak

⅔ cup firmly packed brown sugar
⅔ cup V-8 juice or other brand vegetable juice
⅔ cup low-sodium soy sauce
½ cup olive oil
4 cloves garlic, chopped

2 tablespoons chili powder
¼ teaspoon ground cumin
½ cup chili sauce
¼ teaspoon ground allspice
1 (3-pound) beef flank steak

In a large bowl, combine the brown sugar, V-8 juice, soy sauce, olive oil, garlic, chili powder, cumin, chili sauce, and allspice. Whisk together until blended. Pour half into a large zip-top plastic bag. Add the steak, seal the bag, and turn to coat well. Refrigerate for at least 8 hours or overnight. Cover and refrigerate the remaining marinade.

When ready to cook, remove the steak from the bag and discard the marinade. Heat a grill to 400 to 500 degrees. Grill the steak about 8 minutes on each side. Slice the steak very thinly. Heat the reserved marinade to serve with the steak.

Makes 4 to 6 servings.

Drunken Steaks

4 rib eye steaks
4 tablespoons whiskey or brandy
2 tablespoons soy sauce
1 tablespoon dark brown sugar
Pepper

Make a few cuts along the edge of the steaks and place in a shallow dish.

In a bowl mix the whiskey or brandy, soy sauce, brown sugar, and pepper to taste, stirring until the sugar has dissolved. Pour the liquid over the steak, cover the dish, and marinate in the refrigerator for at least 3 to 4 hours.

Preheat the grill to high heat in one zone and medium heat in another zone.

Grill the steaks on oiled grates over the hot zone for about 2 minutes on each side. Then move them to the cooler zone and cook for another 5 to 10 minutes, until cooked to your desired doneness.

Makes 4 servings.

Barbecued Pot Roast

2 tablespoons vegetable oil

3 to 5 pounds brisket of beef

3 cups sliced yellow onions

3 to 4 cloves garlic, minced

1 (8-ounce) can tomato sauce

4 tablespoons firmly packed brown sugar

¼ cup chili sauce

¼ cup cider vinegar

2 tablespoons Worcestershire sauce

Heat the oil in a Dutch oven, and brown the brisket in the oil. When lightly browned on both sides, add the onions and garlic. When the onions begin to brown, add the tomato sauce and ¼ cup water. Cover and cook over low heat for 45 minutes. Check occasionally to be sure the water has not evaporated. Add another ¼ cup water if necessary. Turn the meat about every 20 minutes to keep it from becoming too brown or sticking to the pan.

Add the brown sugar, chili sauce, vinegar, and Worcestershire sauce, and cook, covered, for 1 ½ hours, adding more water if needed, in small increments to avoid making the barbecue too soupy. At this point, the meat should be tender. Remove the meat from the Dutch oven, and slice very thinly. Continue to cook the sauce until it is thick. Return the meat to the sauce, and cook until the meat is well coated with sauce and warm enough to serve.

Makes 6 to 8 servings.

Grilled Tenderloin with Gingered Jezebel Sauce

Marinade and Meat:

½ cup light soy sauce

2 tablespoons firmly packed dark brown sugar

2 green onions, chopped

2 tablespoons sherry (optional)

Fresh rosemary (optional)

3 pounds pork tenderloin

Jezebel Sauce:

⅔ cup pineapple preserves

⅓ cup apple jelly

2 tablespoons prepared horseradish

1 tablespoon grated fresh ginger

FOOD SAFETY TIP

#43

Don't serve leftovers that are more than three days old.

Combine the soy sauce, brown sugar, onions, sherry, and rosemary in a shallow dish or a zip-top bag. Add the pork and allow it to marinate in the refrigerator for at least 20 minutes.

While the pork is marinating, prepare the sauce. Melt the preserves and jelly over low heat in a saucepan. Stir in the horseradish and ginger.

Preheat a grill to medium-high heat.

Remove the meat from the dish, and discard the marinade. Grill the pork for about 25 minutes, or until the internal temperature reaches 155°. Turn once, basting with ½ cup sauce. Grill for another 5 to 10 minutes, or until the center temperature reaches 160°. Slice and serve the pork with the remaining sauce and fresh rosemary.

Makes 6 servings.

Honey-Glazed Pork Chops

4 pork loin chops

Salt and pepper

4 tablespoons honey

4 tablespoons orange juice

2 tablespoons olive oil

1-inch piece gingerroot, grated

Preheat the grill to medium-hot. (If preparing the glaze on the grill, preheat the grill to low heat and turn it up to medium-hot when the glaze is finished.)

Season the pork chops with salt and pepper to taste and set aside. Combine in a small pan the honey, orange juice, oil, and ginger; heat the mixture on low heat, stirring constantly until the ingredients are blended.

Place the pork chops on oiled grates and cook for about 5 minutes on each side. Brush the chops with the glaze and cook for another 3 to 4 minutes on each side, basting often, until done.

Makes 4 servings.

Short Ribs of Beef Braised with Burgundy Wine

6 pounds beef short ribs, cut into serving-size pieces

½ cup all-purpose flour

⅓ cup bacon fat or vegetable oil

Salt and pepper

1 carrot, finely chopped

1 rib celery, finely chopped

¼ teaspoon dried savory

½ cup beef broth

1 ¼ cups red cooking wine or Burgundy

FOOD SAFETY TIP

#38

Always thoroughly clean your grill before each use.

Preheat the oven to 300º.

Dredge the short ribs in the flour. Heat the bacon fat in a large skillet, and lightly brown the meat. Season with salt and pepper to taste. Spread the carrots and celery over the bottom of a large, ovenproof dish, and sprinkle with the savory. Place the short ribs over the vegetables in a single layer. Combine the broth and wine in a medium-size saucepan, heat until warm, and then pour the mix over the ribs. Cover with foil and cook for 3 hours, or until the beef is tender.

Makes 6 to 8 servings.

Sweet-and-Sour Spare Ribs

2 quarts sauerkraut

2 cups firmly packed brown sugar

1 large onion, diced

1 large apple, cored and diced (skin on)

2 pounds pork ribs

Preheat the oven to 350º.

In a large roaster, combine the sauerkraut, brown sugar, onion, and apple. Add enough water to reach the top of the sauerkraut. Place the ribs on top. Cover and cook for 4 hours. Check occasionally to be sure the water has not evaporated, and add more water, 1 cup at a time, if needed. Uncover the ribs and cook for 1 additional hour.

Makes 6 to 8 servings.

Grilled Brats

10 bratwurst sausages (about 2 pounds)

2 onions, chopped

2 cans beer

10 crusty Kaiser-style rolls, split in half

Brown mustard

Heat the grill to medium.

Place the brats in a large pot. Add the onions, beer, and enough water to cover the brats. Bring to a simmer over medium heat. Reduce the heat to medium-low and simmer gently for 15 to 20 minutes. Be sure not to let the liquid boil (the brats might burst). Using tongs, remove the brats from the liquid. Oil the grill grate. Place the brats on the grate and cook, turning every few minutes, for 10 to 15 minutes or until nicely browned and sizzling. Place the brats in the rolls and serve immediately with mustard.

Makes 5 to 10 servings.

Bratwurst Potato Skillet Dinner

2 teaspoons vegetable oil

2 medium potatoes, sliced

2 fully cooked bratwurst links

1 small onion, chopped

⅓ cup chopped green bell pepper

2 tablespoons soy sauce

1 tablespoon orange juice

½ teaspoon dried basil

¼ teaspoon salt

⅛ teaspoon pepper

In a heavy skillet, heat the oil over medium heat. Cook the potatoes until they are lightly browned and crisp-tender, about 6 minutes. Add the bratwurst, onion, and green bell pepper. Stirring occasionally, cook until the vegetables are crisp-tender and heated through, 5 to 10 minutes. Combine the soy sauce, orange juice, basil, salt, and pepper in a small bowl. Stir the sauce mixture into the meat and vegetables, and heat through.

Makes 2 servings.

Grilled Turkey Cheeseburgers

Tomato Mayonnaise:

¼ cup sun-dried tomatoes, packed in oil

2 teaspoons cider vinegar

1 tablespoon water

¼ cup light mayonnaise

1 strip bacon, cooked and crumbled

Burgers:

1 plus 1 tablespoons olive oil

1 large shallot or 6 green onions, chopped

½ teaspoon poultry seasoning

½ teaspoon salt

½ teaspoon pepper

¼ cup bread crumbs, made from day-old bread

1 ½ pounds ground turkey

5 ounces extra-sharp Cheddar cheese, sliced

4 deluxe burger buns or Kaiser rolls

To prepare the mayonnaise, purée the tomatoes, vinegar, and water in a food processor or blender. Stir in the mayonnaise and crumbled bacon. Refrigerate until ready to serve. (The mayonnaise can be made ahead.)

To make the burgers, heat 1 tablespoon of oil, and sauté the shallot until light golden. Stir in the poultry seasoning, salt, and pepper. In a large bowl, combine the onions with the bread crumbs and turkey. Divide the meat mixture into eight equal portions, and shape into flat patties. Place the cheese slices on top of four of the patties. Cover with the remaining four patties. Pinch the edges to secure the cheese inside the meat. Heat the remaining 1 tablespoon oil in a skillet, and gently cook the burgers until the centers are no longer pink (about 4 minutes per side over medium-high heat).

Serve on toasted buns with the tomato mayonnaise and your favorite greens.

Makes 4 servings.

Honey Pecan Salmon

¼ cup extra virgin olive oil

3 tablespoons honey, plus additional for drizzling

4 (4- to 6-ounce) salmon fillets

1 ½ cups well-chopped pecans

½ tablespoon dried parsley or
1 ½ tablespoons chopped fresh parsley

Salt and pepper

Preheat the grill to high heat.

Mix the olive oil with 3 tablespoons honey in a medium-size
bowl. Dip each fillet in the honey
mixture, and then roll and press it
in the pecans. Place the salmon
on a prepared grill. Sprinkle with
the parsley and salt and pepper
to taste. Drizzle a bit more honey
over each fillet. Cook for about
10 minutes, or until the fish flakes
with a fork.

Makes 4 servings.

Creole Jambalaya

2 tablespoons butter
¾ cup chopped onion
½ cup chopped celery
¼ cup chopped green bell pepper
1 tablespoon chopped parsley
1 clove garlic, minced
2 cups cubed, fully cooked ham
1 (28-ounce) can diced tomatoes, not drained
1 (10 ½-ounce) can beef broth
1 beef broth can of water
1 cup uncooked long grain rice
1 teaspoon sugar
½ teaspoon dried crushed thyme leaves
½ teaspoon chili powder
½ teaspoon pepper
1 ½ pounds raw shrimp, peeled and deveined

Melt the butter in a Dutch oven. Add the onion, celery, green pepper, parsley, and garlic. Cover and cook until tender. Add the ham, tomatoes, broth, water, rice, sugar, thyme, chili powder, and pepper. Cover and simmer until the rice is tender, about 25 minutes. Add the shrimp and simmer until the shrimp are cooked through, about 10 minutes.

Makes 6 to 8 servings.

Red Enchiladas

1 pound ground beef

2 cloves garlic, minced

1 small onion, chopped

2 tablespoons salsa, any kind

¾ teaspoon salt

1 plus 1 ½ cups shredded
Cheddar cheese

1 (20-ounce) can red chili sauce,
divided

¼ cup olive oil

¼ cup all-purpose flour

¼ cup whipping cream

½ teaspoon ground cumin

24 (6-inch) corn tortillas, fried for a
few seconds in oil until limp

Preheat the oven to 350°.

Cook the ground beef in a large skillet until almost completely done, and then add the garlic and onion. Cook for a few minutes together. Drain the fat. Add the salsa, salt, 1 cup cheese, and 2 tablespoons chili sauce. Mix well and set aside.

In a saucepan, heat the olive oil and add the flour. Mix well and cook until bubbly, about 3 minutes. Add the remaining chili sauce, the whipping cream, and cumin. Cook for about 5 minutes, or until thick. Pour 1 cup of this sauce over the bottom of a 13 x 9-inch baking dish.

Use two limp tortillas (slightly overlapped) for each enchilada. Fill each enchilada with 2 to 3 tablespoons meat filling. Roll into a long cylinder. Place the rolled, filled tortillas in a snug row, lining the bottom of the baking dish. Spoon the remaining sauce evenly over the top. Cover with foil and bake for 40 minutes. Uncover and sprinkle with the remaining 1 ½ cups cheese. Bake for 5 minutes longer.

Makes 6 to 12 servings.

Mexican Casserole

½ cup cooked brown rice

1 (11-ounce) can sweet corn, drained

1 (14½-ounce) can stewed tomatoes

1 (4-ounce) can green chiles, diced

1 (16-ounce) can pinto beans, drained

½ green bell pepper and ½ red bell pepper, chopped

1 garlic clove, chopped

½ medium onion, chopped

1 rib celery, chopped

½ pound cooked, lean ground beef

2 tablespoons chili powder

Tabasco (optional)

Low-fat shredded cheese

Reduced-fat sour cream (optional)

Preheat the oven to 350º.

Mix the rice, corn, tomatoes, green chiles, beans, peppers, garlic, onion, celery, ground beef, chili powder, and Tabasco to taste if using, and put in a 9 by 13-inch casserole dish. Top with the cheese. Bake about 10 minutes, or until the cheese is melted. When serving, top with the sour cream, if desired. Note: Vegetables will be crunchy.

Makes 12 servings.

One-Dish-Meal Casserole

1 pound ground beef

2 tablespoons cooking oil

½ cup chopped onion

1 (8-ounce) can tomato sauce

2 ½ cups hot water

2 cups egg noodles, uncooked

½ teaspoon chili powder

1 ½ teaspoons salt

¼ teaspoon pepper

2 teaspoons Worcestershire sauce

1 cup grated sharp Cheddar cheese

1 (15-ounce) can cream-style corn

Preheat the oven to 350°.

Brown the ground beef in the oil. Stir together the beef, onion, tomato sauce, hot water, noodles, chili powder, salt, pepper, Worcestershire sauce, cheese, and corn. Spoon the mixture into a 9 by 13-inch baking pan. Bake for 40 to 50 minutes, or until the noodles are tender.

Makes 12 servings.

Chicken Artichoke Pasta

1 pound chicken breasts
Olive oil for frying
Salt and pepper
12 ounces artichoke hearts
1 cup Manzanilla, or other green olives, cut in half
½ cup black olives, cut in half
1 medium onion, diced
2 zucchini squash, sliced
2 to 4 garlic cloves, minced
8 ounces corkscrew pasta
1 cup Alfredo sauce, or 1 cup Italian dressing

Cut the chicken into bite-size pieces and pan-fry them in olive oil until cooked through. Season with salt and pepper to taste. In a large skillet, sauté the artichoke hearts, olives, onion, squash, and garlic Mix the cooked chicken with the sautéed ingredients.

Cook the pasta according to package directions.

Serve the chicken over the cooked pasta with the Alfredo sauce. (You can also toss with prepared pasta and Italian dressing for a salad you can make ahead.)

Makes 4 to 6 servings.

Pasta Primavera

Tomato Topping:

2 tablespoons olive oil

1 clove minced garlic (about 1 teaspoon)

3 medium red, ripe tomatoes, cut into 1-inch cubes

½ cup chopped fresh basil leaves

½ teaspoon salt

½ teaspoon freshly ground black pepper

Pasta and Alfredo Sauce:

1 pound spaghetti or spaghettini

¼ cup low-sodium chicken broth

½ cup mascarpone cheese

½ cup heavy cream

⅔ cup grated Parmesan cheese

Vegetables:

1 pound broccoli, trimmed and cut into bite-size pieces

2 small zucchini, cut into 2-inch matchstick slices (about 1 ½ cups)

4 asparagus spears, cut in thirds after breaking off their tough ends

2 cups fresh or frozen green peas

1 tablespoon olive oil

½ teaspoon salt

Freshly ground black pepper

½ teaspoon dried red pepper flakes

¼ cup chopped parsley

2 tablespoons butter

Pine nuts (optional)

For the tomato topping, heat the olive oil in a saucepan and add the garlic and tomatoes. Cook about 4 minutes, stirring gently so as not to break up the tomatoes any more than necessary. Stir in the basil, salt, and black pepper.

Cook the spaghetti in boiling water until al dente. Drain well and set aside.

While the spaghetti is cooking, make the Alfredo sauce. Gently heat the chicken broth, mascarpone cheese,

and cream in a very large saucepan; then add the Parmesan cheese and stir until smooth.

For the vegetables, cook the broccoli 3 minutes in boiling water. Add the zucchini and asparagus, and continue cooking until they are crisp-tender, about 2 minutes. Add the peas and cook for 30 seconds if frozen, 1 minute if fresh. Drain the vegetables well.

Heat the olive oil in a large skillet; add the vegetables, salt, black pepper to taste, red pepper flakes, and parsley. Cook 2 minutes, stirring gently, just long enough to heat through. Add the butter and toss gently.

Add the spaghetti to the Alfredo sauce and toss to coat. Add the vegetables, tossing and stirring over very low heat. Serve the spaghetti with the tomato topping. Garnish with pine nuts, if using.

Makes 6 servings.

Chocolate Earthquake Cake

1 box German chocolate cake mix

1 (3 ½-ounce) can sweetened flaked coconut

1 cup chopped nuts

¼ cup butter

8 ounces cream cheese, softened

1 (16-ounce) box confectioners' sugar

Preheat the oven to 350º.

Prepare the cake batter according to package instructions.

Grease a 9 by 12-inch baking pan. Cover the bottom of the pan with the coconut and nuts. Pour the cake batter on top. Melt the butter in a bowl. Add to it the cream cheese and confectioners' sugar. Stir to blend. Spoon over the unbaked batter and bake for 40 to 42 minutes. You can't test for doneness with this sticky cake. The icing sinks to the bottom while baking and makes a gooey white ribbon throughout.

Makes about 24 squares.

Apple Cake

6 to 8 tart apples, depending on size of apples

2 eggs

1 cup sugar plus extra for topping

1 cup milk

½ teaspoon salt

2 teaspoons baking powder

2 cups all-purpose flour

Cinnamon

Butter

Preheat the oven to 350°.

Peel and chop the apples. Beat the eggs in a large bowl. Add the 1 cup sugar and milk, and beat again. Mix the salt, baking powder, and flour, and add to the egg mixture. Beat all together. Pour into two 9-inch greased cake pans or one 9 by 13-inch pan. Cover with the apples. Sprinkle with the additional sugar and the cinnamon and dot with the butter. Bake about 30 minutes.

Makes 10 to 20 slices.

Too Easy Peach Cobbler

1 (29-ounce) can sliced peaches, drained

5 slices white bread

1 ½ cups sugar

2 tablespoons all-purpose flour

1 egg, beaten

1 stick butter, melted

Preheat the oven to 350°.

Place the peaches in a baking dish (8 by 8 inches or larger). Cut the crust from the bread, and cut each slice into five strips. Place the strips over the peaches. Mix the sugar, flour, egg, and butter. Blend well and pour the mix over the bread strips. Bake 35 to 45 minutes or until golden brown.

Makes 9 to 12 servings.

Bittersweet Chocolate Brownies

5 ounces unsweetened chocolate, coarsely chopped

12 tablespoons (1 ½ sticks) unsalted butter, at room temperature

1 ½ cups sugar

2 tablespoons all-purpose flour

6 eggs

Combine the chocolate and butter in a medium bowl. Cover with plastic wrap and place in a microwave oven on medium for 3 minutes. Stir well. Cool to room temperature.

Preheat the oven to 325°.

Place the sugar and flour in a mixer bowl and mix for 30 seconds on low speed. Increase the speed to medium and add the eggs, one at a time, mixing well after each addition. With the mixer on low speed, drizzle in the cooled, melted chocolate mixture. Increase speed to medium, and mix for about 1 minute or until the batter is mousse-like in texture.

Lightly oil an 8 by 9-inch or a 9-inch-square baking pan. Pour the batter into the prepared baking pan and spread it evenly with a rubber spatula. Bake on the center rack of the oven for 30 to 35 minutes, or until the center is just set. Cool on a wire rack.

Makes about 12 squares.

Hawaiian Bars

Crust:
2 cups all-purpose flour

1 cup sugar

1 cup butter, softened

Filling:
16 ounces cream cheese, softened

6 tablespoons sugar

4 tablespoons milk

2 eggs

2 teaspoons vanilla extract

1 (16-ounce) can crushed pineapple, drained

Topping:
2 cups flaked coconut

2 tablespoons butter, melted

Preheat the oven to 350°.

For the crust, mix together the flour, sugar, and butter until well blended. Press into an ungreased 9 x 13-inch baking dish. Bake for 10 minutes. Set aside while making the filling.

For the filling, combine the cream cheese, sugar, milk, eggs, and vanilla in a large mixing bowl, and beat together until very smooth. Stir in the pineapple until well blended. Spoon the filling over the cake.

For the topping, sprinkle the coconut evenly over the filling. Drizzle the butter evenly over the coconut. Bake the cake for about 25 minutes, until the coconut is lightly browned. Cool and serve.

Makes about 24 squares.

Peanut Butter Fudge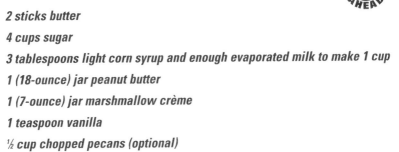

2 sticks butter

4 cups sugar

3 tablespoons light corn syrup and enough evaporated milk to make 1 cup

1 (18-ounce) jar peanut butter

1 (7-ounce) jar marshmallow crème

1 teaspoon vanilla

½ cup chopped pecans (optional)

Melt the butter in a medium saucepan. Add the sugar, syrup, and milk. Bring to a boil and cook 5 minutes. Remove from the stove. Add the peanut butter, marshmallow crème, vanilla, and pecans if using. Pour into a greased 9 by 13-inch pan. Cool and cut into squares.

Makes about 24 squares.

Caramel Corn

2 cups brown sugar

1 cup butter

½ cup light corn syrup

1 teaspoon salt

1 teaspoon baking soda

7 ½ quarts popped popcorn

Preheat the oven to 200°.

In a saucepan, heat the sugar, butter, corn syrup, and salt. Stir occasionally. When the mixture comes to a full boil, cook for 5 minutes. Remove from the heat and stir in the baking soda. Pour the caramel mixture over the popcorn and mix until evenly coated. Bake for 1 hour in a large, greased roasting pan, stirring every 15 minutes.

Makes 7 ½ quarts popcorn.

Drinks

Of course, food isn't the only thing you're whipping up outside the track. You need something to wash it all down. Beer, wine, soft drinks, and fruit juices are the most common tailgating beverages—and you don't have to do anything to make those—but you should spice up your tailgate party with a fun drink now and then.

Regardless of what you're drinking for fun and taste, be sure to drink lots of water. It's important for staying cool and hydrated.

Drinks

57 Chevy with Hawaiian Plates

1 ounce vodka
1 ounce amaretto
1 ounce Grand Marnier
Pineapple juice

Combine the vodka, amaretto, and Grand Marnier in a cocktail mixer and shake well. Put some ice cubes in a pitcher and pour in the mixed liquors. Fill the pitcher with pineapple juice and stir.

Makes 8 to 12 servings.

Fast Fruit Punch

1 (12-ounce) can frozen lemonade
1 (12-ounce) can frozen orange juice
1 (46-ounce) can pineapple juice
1 (10-ounce) package frozen strawberries
1 (2-liter) bottle ginger ale

Separately, make the lemonade and orange juice according to the instructions on the cans. Mix them together in a large pitcher or a punch bowl. Add the pineapple juice and then stir in the strawberries. Stir in the ginger ale just prior to serving.

Makes 25 to 35 servings.

Ultimate Tailgater's Bloody Mary

Ultimate Tailgater's Bloody Mary Mix
Vodka

This recipe is a bit of self-promotion for the Ultimate Tailgater's Bloody Mary Mix, but it's very easy to make and is a spicy drink to get you going. It's also a good drink to scale to any size crowd. Just mix 3 to 4 parts Bloody Mary mix with 1 part vodka, stir, and serve chilled.

(To learn where you can find Ultimate Tailgater's Bloody Mary Mix, visit theultimatetailgater.com and click on the link.)

Just Peachy Margaritas

6 ounces tequila
3 ounces Peach Schnapps
5 ounces sour mix
Ice

Combine the tequila, Peach Schnapps, and sour mix in a blender, and mix for about 15 seconds. Add the ice to fill the blender most of the way, and mix to the consistency of your choice.

Makes 4 to 6 servings.

Orange Crush Smoothie

1 quart orange sherbet

2 cups orange juice

1 cup milk

Whipped cream (optional)

Combine the sherbet, orange juice, and milk in a blender and blend until smooth. Pour into glasses and, if desired, top with a dollop of whipped cream.

Makes 2 to 3 servings.

Track Tea

1 gallon water

4 large tea bags

6 sprigs of fresh mint

2 ⅔ cups sugar

1 ½ cups orange juice

1 cup lemon juice

1 (1-liter) bottle ginger ale

Boil the water, add the tea bags, and steep for 10 minutes. Remove the bags and add the mint and sugar. Stir until the sugar has dissolved. Remove from the heat and let cool. Pour in the orange and lemon juices and refrigerate until cold. Just prior to serving, stir in the ginger ale.

Makes 25 to 30 servings.

Bailey's Coffee

2 ounces Bailey's Irish whiskey
Hot coffee
Whipped cream

Pour the Bailey's into a coffee mug, followed by the coffee, and stir. Add the whipped cream to the top, or stir it into the drink.

Makes 1 serving.

Warm-Me-Up Punch

2 ½ cups orange juice
5 ½ cups apple juice
¼ cup honey
2 tablespoons lemon juice
1 ½ tablespoons ground cinnamon

Combine the orange and apple juices in a saucepan and warm over medium heat until hot, but be careful not to let the mixture boil. Remove from the heat and stir in the honey, lemon juice, and cinnamon. Serve warm.

Makes 8 servings.

FOOD SAFETY TIP

#86

Don't let food sit out in the summer heat for more than two hours. If the temperature is 90 degrees Fahrenheit or more, cut that to one hour.

Resources

Throughout this book I've talked about all the stuff you need to throw the ultimate racing tailgate party. What I haven't told you is where to get all this stuff if you can't find it where you live. Now I will.

For news and information about racing and your favorite drivers, your first stop should be the racing league Web sites. For additional insights and updates, here are a few other sites that do a good job of keeping up with racing.

RACING LEAGUES
NASCAR (all series)—nascar.com
IHRA—ihra.com
NHRA—nhra.com
IRL—indycar.com
Champ Car—champcarworldseries.com

OTHER INFORMATION SITES
insiderracingnews.com
motorsport.com
nascar.about.com
racingjunky.com
racingone.com
thatsracin.com
topix.net/racing

When you're at the track for NASCAR races, you can listen in on the drivers and pit crews with a radio scanner. Scanners are available online and at any number of electronics stores. Just as important is getting current frequencies for the drivers. These sites have driver frequencies and can hook you up with a scanner and accessories.

mphmotorsports.com/scannersWC.htm

nascar.about.com/od/racefrequencies

nationalradiodata.com (click on "Racing Frequencies")

racescanners.com

racingjunky.com (click on "Scanner Frequencies" on the left side of the home page)

speedwayscanner.com

You're an adult. You don't need me to tell you where to go to get a grill and supplies. You can find them all over the place. What you may not know is where to go to compare grills to help you make the right buying decision. These sites offer great research and recommendations.

bbq.about.com/od/grills/index.htm?terms=grills

consumersearch.com/www/sports_and_leisure/gas-grill
reviews/index.html

In some cities, it can be hard to find racing-themed apparel and gear beyond the basics. So to show your spirit in textile, try some of these sites.

atthetrackracing.com/default.aspx

basspro.com (click on "Tailgate Zone")

http://stores.musictoday.com/store/dept.asp?band_id=1142&dept_id=872
3&sfid=2

speedgear.com

speedzoneracestore.com

sportsfanoutlet.com/nascar.htm

thenitrotimes.com/teamshops

You're throwing a party out there, so you need decorations and party gear, right? Well, these folks can help you out with that.

bulkpartysupplies.com

nascar-racing.character-party-supplies.com

partycity.com

partypro.com

partythemeshop.com (search keyword: "party themes")

racechex.com

You can find more links at theultimatetailgater.com; just click on "Lists & Links."

Track Guides

When you add up all the tracks that host the various levels of NASCAR, IHRA, NHRA, IRL, and Champ Car races in the country, you get a handful shy of 300, each with its own rules and regulations about what tailgaters can do. And every track is in this book.

The icon key below will help you navigate the Track Guides, which also include contact information. When this book was printed, all the information in these Track Guides was accurate. But of course, things can change, so it's always a good idea to check with the track or its Web site before you leave. If you have any questions about the track rules, call the number provided for that track for clarification.

Every track has a few rules: pets must be kept on a leash in tailgating areas and are not allowed in the stands or near the track (although some tracks prohibit pets altogether); only licensed drivers may drive 4x4s, golf carts, and similar personal vehicles on track property; and no weapons, drugs, or fireworks are allowed on the property. But you knew that last one. Didn't you?

Finally, since there will be about 6 million or so fans at NASCAR Nextel Cup races this year, I've also included for those tracks icons and rules for what you can take into the stands while watching the race. After all, it's a long walk to your car and back.

CAMPING ICON GUIDE

RVs may park overnight before or after event.

Number of days you can tailgate before the event.

Number of days you can tailgate after the event.

Number of hours you can tailgate before the event.

Number of hours you can tailgate after the event.

Shuttle service available to/from tailgating area.

Infield parking available.

Camping allowed.

Canopies may be erected.

Decorations allowed.

Tailgating furniture allowed.

Grills allowed.

Pets on leash allowed.

Electric hookup available.

Venue offers visible security in tailgating areas.

Medical or first aid available.

Alcohol allowed.

RVs allowed.

Open campfires allowed.

Personal motor vehicles allowed.

$
Parking is no more than $30 per day per vehicle.

$$
Parking is between $30 and $50 per day per vehicle.

$$$
Parking is more than $50 per day per vehicle.

GRANDSTAND ICON GUIDE

Alcohol allowed.

Personal video recording devices allowed.

Personal bags allowed.

Coolers allowed.

Food and beverages allowed.

Abilene Star Dodge Dragstrip

5601 W. Stamford, Abilene, TX 79603

(325) 673-7223

IHRA

Abilene has 500 paid-parking spots. Tailgating allowed in 30 to 35 spaces along track's edge. Parking runs $5 to $15 per day, per person (not vehicle) depending on event. Most races are one-day events. Golf cart use allowed for fans 16 years and older. No other personal motorized vehicles; no bicycles or skateboards. No glass or open fires, decorations must not obscure sightlines. Track is just off the I-20 highway. Staff's very friendly.

Ace Speedway

3401 Altamahaw Racetrack Rd., Altamahaw, NC 27244

(336) 585-1200

acespeedway.com

NASCAR Regional, Dodge Weekly

This track did not provide additional information about tailgating or race-day regulations.

Adams County Speedway

Adams County Fairgrounds

12th St. at John St., Corning, IA 50841

(641) 322-4184

acspeedway.com

Dodge Weekly

Speedway has 2,000 day-only parking spaces. Parking included in admission fee. No open fires, alcohol, or glass allowed on facility property. Personal vehicles are allowed in parking area. Speedway has VIP deck; space must be reserved on an annual basis. All bags will be inspected before entering gates.

Adirondack International Speedway

8712 Cut Off Rd., Lowville, NY 13367

(315) 346-7223

adirondackspeedway.com

NASCAR Regional

Speedway has 10 acres overnight camping available. If full, several campgrounds and state parks nearby—check Web site for specifics. Personal motorized vehicles, bikes allowed; no glass, no open fires. Wood fires in approved fire rings okay, bring own wood. Must have fire extinguisher. Pet owners must provide license, rabies certificate. Swimming, wading not permitted in streams and ponds.

Alabama International Dragway

1245 Crump Rd., Steele, AL 35987

(256) 538-7223

alabamainternationaldragway.com

IHRA

Dragway has 2,000 spaces for day-use parking. Parking included in admission fee. No overnight parking allowed. Tailgating and event parking starts at 5 p.m., ends 1 hour after race's conclusion. Open fires allowed if contained in a pit. Keep pets leashed. No personal vehicles allowed in parking areas or pit. Shade canopies and tailgating furniture not allowed. Friday night is "Moonlight Madness," when all ladies are admitted free from 9 p.m. to 1 a.m.

Alaska Raceway Park

Mile 10.4 Old Glenn Hwy., Palmer, AK 99645

(907) 746-7223

akracewaypark.com

IHRA

Park has 150 overnight RV sites, 800 day parking spaces. Camping, spectator parking both free. Pit parking $10 for RVs, cars $5. Campers can arrive 1 day before 3-day events, or call office for arrangements. Leave day after race, or talk to management. Spectators, crew, drivers wear official wristbands at all times. No wristband means expulsion from event. No personal vehicles during event. No alcohol during races. Alcohol okay after day's race is over. Lounge on premises serves beer and wine. Due to Park's unique location, management willing to help long distance RV travelers with travel concerns. Park sits at base of Pioneer Peak, Knik River—worth trip for scenery alone.

Albuquerque National Dragway

5700 Bobby Foster Rd. SE, Albuquerque, NM 87112
Event line: (505) 323-7077, Track line: (505) 873-2684
abqdragway.com
NHRA

Dragway has more than 600 parking spots. Camping, day parking free with admission to event. All camping dry; no hookups. Other campsite locations nearby. No personal motorized vehicles; bikes okay. No glass or open fires. Alcohol allowed, but strongly discouraged. Be discreet. Bringing pets strongly discouraged due to area's intense heat. Dragway proud of strong family atmosphere; emphasis on safety and well-behaved fun.

Altamont Motorsports Park

17001 Midway Rd., Tracy, CA 95376
(925) 371-7223
altamontracing.com
NASCAR Regional, Dodge Weekly

Park has 2,000 day-only parking spaces; no overnight camping. Parking included in admission price. Personal vehicles are fine in parking lots. No alcohol, open fires, or pets allowed on property. No glass allowed. Coolers and backpacks not allowed in grandstands. Leave them in your vehicle.

Angleton Raceway

27250 FM 2004, Angleton, TX

(979) 849-3633

angletonraceway.com

IHRA

Angleton has 40 acres of camping, day parking. Both parking and RV camping free. No tent camping. No personal motorized vehicles or bikes. No open fires. Raceway very family-centered, bring everybody. Angleton's racers young as 12 years, old as 80 years.

Area 51 Dragway

Will Rogers Rd., Roswell, NM 88203

(505) 627-3968

area51dragway.com

NHRA

Dragway has 3,000 parking spaces. Campers can arrive day before race, stay until conclusion of event. Parking and camping both included in admission price. Tailgating and day parking start at noon, end 1 hour after end of race. Personal vehicles not allowed. Shade canopies, tents, and tailgating furniture not allowed. Open fires must be kept in fire pits. Pets must be leashed. On-site showers available.

Atco Raceway

1000 Jackson Rd., Atco, NJ 08004

(856) 768-2167

atcorace.com

NHRA

Raceway has 1,500 day-only parking spaces; no overnight camping. Personal vehicles allowed in parking lots. No glass or open fires.

Atlanta Dragway

500 E. Ridgeway Rd., Commerce, GA 30529

(706) 335-2301

atlantadragway.com

NHRA

Track occasionally rents to outside promoters for special events. During special events, promoters set separate prices for parking, camping. During normal events, no camping available, parking free. Three outside campgrounds within 20-minute drive. Shuttles available during NHRA Powerade Series. In tailgating areas, no personal motorized vehicles or bicycles; no tailgating furniture or grills; no alcohol inside facility. Convenience store next to track.

Atlanta Motor Speedway

1500 Tara Pl., Hampton, GA 30228

Ticket office: (770) 946-4211

atlantamotorspeedway.com

Nextel Cup, Busch Series, Craftsman Trucks

Camping: Speedway has 840 acres parking. Day parking free. Unreserved camping $40 first-come, first-served; infield camping from $45 to $70 (not including gate admission); reserved camping from $90 to year's camping for $7,990 at Turn One Trackside. Reserved parking available close to track $75. RVs can park up to a week before race day. No open fires, external sound systems, golf carts, alcohol in family campgrounds or family grandstand section. **Grandstand:** No umbrellas, strollers, or glass containers in grandstands. Cooler size limit 14x14x14 inches. Shuttle service available through vroomz.com. Check Speedway's Web site for list of nearby hotels.

Atmore Dragway

1301 Curtis Rd., Atmore, AL 36502

(251) 583-6797

atmoredragway.com

IHRA

Dragway has 10,000 total parking spaces. Overnight camping during big events only; no hookups. During big events, RV and tent camping allowed first to last day of event. Personal motorized vehicles okay, no bikes. Tailgaters charged a fee for larger, oversized grills or smokers. Dragway doesn't sell alcohol, BYOB allowed. No glass allowed, no tailgating furniture allowed.

Auto Club Dragway at California Speedway

9300 Cherry Ave., Fontana, CA 93250

(909) 429-5060 or (909) 429-5061

californiaspeedway.com

NHRA

See **California Speedway** entry for track details.

Auto Club Famoso Raceway

33559 Famoso Rd., McFarland, CA 93250

(661) 399-5351

famosoraceway.com

NHRA

Famoso has 2,000 all-purpose parking spaces. Parking fees included in ticket price. Overnight parking allowed on event days only. Tailgating and day parking starts 1 hour before race, ends 1 hour afterwards. Personal vehicles allowed in parking areas. No open fires; pets must be leashed.

Auto Club Raceway at Pomona

2780 Fairplex Dr., Pomona, CA 91768
Racing information: (909) 593-7010
Camping reservations: (909) 623-3111
fairplex.com
NHRA

Parking area run by fairground. No strict rules on arrival or departure times. RVs, other oversized vehicles $45 day or overnight. Car parking runs $8–$25 depending on proximity to track. In parking and camping areas, no personal motorized vehicles or bikes; no canopies or camping tents; no tailgating furniture allowed. The Sheraton Fairplex is located on the premises.

Bandimere Speedway

3051 S. Rooney Rd., Morrison, CO 80465
(303) 697-6001
NHRA

Speedway has 8,000 spaces for day parking. Overnight camping allowed during multiday events only; no hookups. Campers can arrive one day before race during multiday events. Day parking for cars runs $5–$10. RV, bus parking $50 for day only; RV and car camping fee $250 for multiday event weekend. If sold out, try Bear Creek Lake State Park campground, ½ mile away. No personal motorized vehicles or bikes; no tailgating furniture or alcohol. No decorations or open fires.

Barona One-Eighth Mile Dragstrip

1750 Wildcat Canyon Rd., Lakeside, CA 92040

(619) 993-0272

baronadrags.com

NHRA

Barona has more than 2,500 total parking spots. RVs park or camp for $25 per day. Cars park free. Golf carts allowed; no other personal vehicles. Charcoal grills allowed, not gas. No oversized grills allowed. Track has permanent restrooms with running water. Casino located 4 miles away.

Beaver Springs Dragway

89 Race Track Lane, Beaver Springs, PA 17812

(717) 248-7676

beaversprings.com

IHRA

Dragway has 900 parking spaces. Overnight camping on Memorial Day and Labor Day weekends only. Gray Squirrel Lodge campground 6 miles away. Day parking for cars, RVs free. Camping $10 per night. No personal motorized vehicles; bikes okay. Alcohol limited to one six-pack per person; no kegs. No glass. Pets stay on leash; no large, aggressive breeds. Facility provides conservative family atmosphere—partying, rowdy behavior prohibited. Police check ID, eject drunk or unruly guests.

Beech Bend Raceway Park

798 Beech Bend Rd., Bowling Green, KY 42101

(270) 781-7634

beechbend.com

NHRA

Park combines raceway, amusement park, water park, campground, and meeting facility. Campground has 250 spaces for RVs and more than 500 tent camping spaces; all have full hookups. More RV spaces available trackside during NHRA events, but no hookups. Campground spaces run $25–$30 per day, $150–$200 per week. Prices (and hookups) same for tent camping. Trackside camping prices vary by event. In campground, RVs arrive, depart whenever. Trackside RVs arrive day of event, leave at event's end same day. Personal motorized vehicles allowed in park, bicycles in campground. Open fires allowed in campground area. Alcohol fine, though local county dry—BYOB.

Beech Ridge Motor Speedway

70 Holmes Rd., Scarborough, ME 04074

(207) 885-5800

beechridge.com

Dodge Weekly

Speedway has 1,000 parking spaces. All parking, camping free. Two campgrounds in Scarborough, 10 minutes away; more in Old Orchard Beach, 15 minutes away. Motorcycles, bikes allowed; no other personal vehicles. Alcohol fine, but no exposed containers. Beech Ridge enforces family-friendly atmosphere. Track located in beach community.

Ben Bruce Memorial Airpark Raceway "The Dale"

2364 FM 105 S., Evadale, TX 77615

(409) 276-1910

evadaleraceway.com

IHRA

The Dale has open lot parking, plus 1 mile roadside parking, dependent on weather. No RVs; no overnight camping. Personal vehicles, bikes fine except in pit area. Raceway in dry county—no alcohol.

Bluegrass Raceway Park

674 Wells Rd., Owingsville, KY 40360

(606) 674-3987

bluegrassracewaypark.com

NHRA

Park has 250 camping, parking spaces total. No real limit on arrival or departure. All parking, camping free. All personal vehicles allowed. Park located in dry county; keep alcohol in plain container, unexposed.

Bonanza Raceway

Middle Waitsburg Rd., Walla Walla, WA 99362

(509) 522-4804

bonanzaraceway.com

NHRA

Bonanza has 2,000 parking spaces, day use only. Parking included in admission price. No open fires or glass at track. Pets must be leashed; no glass allowed on property. Hearing protection required for spectators 10 years and under.

Bowman Gray Stadium

1250 S. Martin Luther King Dr., Winston-Salem, NC 27107

(336) 725-5635

ljvm.com

NASCAR Regional, Dodge Weekly

Stadium part of Lawrence Joel Veteran's Memorial Coliseum Complex, owned by city of Winston-Salem. Most stadium parking in open lot with 500 paved spaces, including handicapped. Area accommodates maximum 5,000 cars. No overnight camping or parking. No RV or oversized vehicle parking spaces. Event parking free. Dixie Classic Fairgrounds campground nearby charges $20 per night, including full hookup. No tailgating furniture or alcohol; no stickers as decoration. Only gas grills allowed; oversized gas grills okay. No open fires or pets. Fans leave by 11 p.m. Track trivia: Stadium was first paved NASCAR track, now longest running weekly race track.

Bradenton Motorsports Park

21000 SR 64, Bradenton, FL 34202

(941) 748-1320

bradentonmotorsports.com

NHRA

Park has 1,000 day-parking spaces. RV camping allowed only for weekend events; 400 spaces available. No tent camping. Park's Web site lists two nearby campgrounds. Parking, camping free to all spectators. Cars, RVs can arrive 8 a.m. (race times vary widely). Bicycles allowed; no motorized personal vehicles. No alcohol, oversized grills, or tailgating furniture.

Brainerd International Raceway (BIR)

5523 Birchdale Rd., Brainerd, MN 56401

(218) 824-7220

brainerdracewayandresort.com

NHRA

BIR has 164 full-service RV sites with full hookups, located by lake. Family campground well patrolled. Rustic camping also available. Camping, day parking usually free; major events $10. Pit-side parking has up to 100 spaces; otherwise, park along 3-mile roadside stretch. Continuous shuttle throughout parking area. All motorized personal vehicles allowed; $10 advance, $15 at gate. No glass; pets fine. Contest held for best-dressed campsite.

Bremerton Raceway

Near 6000 Old Clifton Rd., Port Orchard, WA 98367

(360) 674-2280

bremertonraceway.com

NHRA

Bremerton has about 15 acres parking. Overnight camping on Friday, Saturday only. Overnight parking $5 for weekend. Two nearby state parks offer camping. Day parking free. No canopies or camping tents; no tailgating furniture or decorations; no alcohol or open fires; no pets; no personal motorized vehicles. Riding bicycle before or after race okay. Small gas or charcoal grills allowed. Must dispose of coals off-site. Must be a spectator or participant to tailgate. Family atmosphere only.

Bristol Motor Speedway

151 Speedway Blvd., Bristol, TN 37620

Guest Services: (423) 989-6933

bristolmotorspeedway.com

Nextel Cup, Busch Series, Craftsman Trucks

Camping: Parking on BMS grounds by permit only. Bristol also operates two free parking areas on St. Rt. 394. Other parking from $10 to $30 per day. Camping prices start $140 per event, to $1,800 per year. No infield camping or parking. No tent camping allowed. No golf carts or ATVs. No open fires, beer kegs, or balls in camp areas. **Grandstand:** In grandstand no horns, umbrellas, folding chairs, glass, or items posing safety hazard. Fans limited to cooler and 1 other carry-in item. Cooler size limit 14 inches all sides. Shuttle available to nearby Food City. Bristol stresses arriving early.

Bullring at Las Vegas Motor Speedway

7000 Las Vegas Blvd. N, Las Vegas, NV 89115

(800) 644-4444

lvms.com

Dodge Weekly

See **Las Vegas Motor Speedway** entry for details.

Bunker Hill Dragstrip

8672 S. 150 W., Bunker Hill, IN 46914

(765) 689-8248

bunkerhillrace.com

NHRA

Dragstrip has 10 acres for general parking, camping. All free. Trackside reserved parking $100 for season. No personal motorized vehicles, no bicycle riding during race. Must be 16 years old to ride bike. No tailgating furniture; no glass. Decorations must be firmly attached, not obstructing view. Pets on leash fine; no large or aggressive breeds. Fires contained in barrel or fire pit okay. Special event admission prices can vary; check Web site.

Byron Dragway

7287 River Rd., Byron, IL 61010

(815) 234-8405

byrondragway.com

IHRA

Dragway has 25 acres for parking, camping. Camping allowed Friday, Saturday nights. Fans arrive as early as 1 p.m. Friday, 8:30 a.m. Saturday, Sunday, and holidays. Parking, camping free. Personal vehicles fine; 5 mph speed limit. No tailgating furniture allowed. No alcohol in pits; otherwise okay. Adjacent to track are 6,000-acre park, 4-star golf course.

California Speedway

9300 Cherry Ave., Fontana, CA 92336

(800) 944-7223

californiaspeedway.com

Nextel Cup, Busch Series, Craftsman Trucks, NASCAR Regional, Champ Car

Camping: Speedway has 30,000 free daytime parking spaces. Bus, limo parking in Lot 7A. RV, tent camping in infield or Napa Street lot only; 1,800 reserved infield sites available. Additional 500 sites at Napa Street lot. Camping $100 for weekend; must have two tickets for Friday and two tickets for Saturday. Infield guests can park extra vehicle overnight in Lot 7 or 8, first-come, first-served. No open fires, glass, personal motorized vehicles. Bikes allowed in camping area. No driving stakes into asphalt. Speedway offers child wristbands, onsite grocery store in infield. **Grandstand:** In grandstand, fans allowed one soft-sided bag or cooler up to 6 x 6 x 12 inches, one plastic bag up to 18 x 18 x 4 inches. No alcohol, glass; no skateboards, scooters, wagons, or personal motorized vehicles. Shuttles available during NASCAR events only.

Capitol Raceway

1451 Capitol Raceway Rd., Crofton, MD 21114

Week Day: (410) 793-0661, Race Day: (410) 721-0782

capitolraceway.com

NHRA

Raceway offers over 1,000 total parking, camping sites. If sold out, KOA campground in Millersville 3 miles away. Campers stay night before race and race night, then leave next day. Parking and camping free. No personal motorized vehicles. No tailgating furniture, glass, or open fires. Pets okay, but no snakes.

Caraway Speedway

2518 Race Track Rd. Ext., Sophia, NC 27350

(336) 629-5803

carawayspeedway.com

NASCAR Regional, Dodge Weekly

Caraway's camping, parking area covers 20 acres. Parking, camping free. No personal motorized vehicles; bicycles okay. No canopies, camping tents, or tailgating furniture. Caraway in dry county; fans bringing own alcohol is fine.

Carolina Dragway

302 Dragstrip Rd., Aiken, SC 29803

(877) 471-RACE

carolinadragway.com

IHRA

Dragway has over 50 acres of general use parking for spectators. Overnight parking allowed race days only. Tailgating, day parking can start first thing in the morning race day, must wrap up 1 hour after race's end. Open fires allowed in approved fire pits. No glass at track. Pets must be leashed. Breakfast served at 7 a.m. Dragway has a playground and is family-friendly.

Cecil County Dragway

1916 Theodore Rd., Rising Sun, MD 21911

(410) 879-1822

cecilcountydragway.com

NHRA

Dragway has about 50 acres parking, camping. Overnight camping only during major multi-day events, no hookups. Parking, camping both free. Personal vehicles okay, but driver must be over 16 years; vehicle must be licensed, registered, with insurance. No alcohol, tailgating furniture, or open fires. No decorations or pets.

Cedar Falls Raceway

6400 W. Bennington Rd., Cedar Falls, IA 50613

(319) 464-2471

cedarfallsraceway.com

IHRA

Raceway has 50 acres parking, camping, 40 RV sites with hookups. Parking, camping free. No hard rules on arrival times, but campers pay spectator fees for all races during time camped. Personal vehicles allowed. All tailgating furniture fine, but must stay inside camp space. Let management know if bringing chairs, tables etc. Pets on leash fine, no large or aggressive breeds.

Champion Raceway

6900 Kershaw Rd., White City, OR 97503

(541) 830-3724 (DRAG)

championraceway.com

NHRA

Raceway has 1,000 day-parking spaces, 200 camping spaces. During major events camping $25 for entire three- to four-day event; otherwise, camping free. No hard rules on campers' arrival time; use common sense. ATVs, golf carts allowed; bikes okay. Golf cart rentals available. No motorcycles, mopeds, etc. No tailgating furniture, decorations, or open fires. Alcohol okay in day parking, but not camping—camping area also pit area.

Cherokee County Motorsports Park

1157 CR 2404, Rusk, TX 75785

(903) 683-4711

cherokeecountymotorsportspark.com

NHRA

Park has room for approximately 2,000 vehicles in open field. Parking, camping both free. Personal vehicles allowed. Whatever campers bring (tent, camping furniture, etc.) campers must take home. No glass; no open fires.

Cherokee Raceway Park

154 Racetrack Rd., Rogersville, TN 37857

(423) 272-2555

cherokeeracewaypark.com

IRHA

Park has 1,500 parking spaces. Overnight camping allowed only the night before event. Personal vehicles not allowed in parking or track areas. No open fires allowed. Alcohol not allowed in parking areas. Keep pets leashed.

Chicagoland Speedway

3200 S. Chicago St., Joliet, IL 64036

(815) 727-7223

chicagolandspeedway.com

Nextel Cup, Busch Series

Camping: RV camping greatly expanded in 2006. Camping runs $550–$2,900. Speedway has 50,000 free day-parking spaces. Bicycles allowed in camping, infield areas only; personal motorized vehicles must have approved decal permit. No wood or uncontained ground fires; no glass; no water guns or balloon launchers; no spotlights, laser pointers, other potentially harmful items. No external sound systems. No pets or tent camping. No scaffolds, temporary canopies, loose lumber, or portable/temporary spectator stands.

Platforms can be no higher than 12 inches above RV. No infield flags, banners higher than RVs. Only 16 people per RV space. Speedway offers nightly movies for kids, concerts for fans. Convenience store also onsite.**Grandstand:** In grandstand, fans can bring unopened bottled water, small bag, seat cushions, camcorder, other personal electronics; no coolers, food, beverages, glass; no items blocking other fans' view. Note: Coolers are allowed for refrigerating medically necessary drugs.

Coastal Plains Dragways

4744 Richlands Hwy., Jacksonville, NC 28540

(910) 455-7223 (RACE)

coastalplainsraceway.com

NHRA

Coastal Plains has 50 acres total parking. Overnight camping only during major events. Parking, camping (when available) free. Golf carts, bicycles allowed; no other personal vehicles. No camping tents, tailgating furniture, or open fires allowed. No glass. Facility includes Coastal Plains Raceway, a ⁵⁄₁₀ mile paved oval track for stock cars.

Colorado National Speedway

4281 Weld County Rd. 10, Dacono, CO 80514

(303) 828-0116

coloradospeedway.com

NASCAR Regional, Dodge Weekly

Speedway offers 50 spaces for motor homes and tailgaters. No overnight parking; day parking free. Motorcycles, mopeds, bikes all allowed. No ATVs or golf carts. No alcohol allowed in parking area; no open fires. Kids under 10 years admitted free. Check Web site for list of hotels, grandstand policy, other information.

Columbus Motor Speedway

1841 Williams Rd., Columbus, OH 43207

(614) 491-1047

columbusspeedway.com

Dodge Weekly

Speedway has 2,000 parking spaces, day parking only. Arrive, depart whenever. No personal vehicles, camping tents, or pets allowed.

Concord Motorsports Park

7940 U.S. Hwy. 601 S., Concord, NC 28025

(704) 782-4221

concordmotorsportpark.com

Dodge Weekly

Park has 25 acres of open space for all parking, camping. Additional 28 spaces at Turn 3; spectators watch race from inside vehicles, tailgating allowed, used from 5:30 p.m. to 1 hour after race ends, one vehicle per space. Turn 3 parking $15 first-come, first-served, available at box office 5:30 p.m. Turn 3 season rental $275 (excludes events by outside promoters). All other parking, camping free. Two week camping limit. Personal vehicles stay outside fence. Decorations fine, but only if affixed to vehicle. Tailgate with outdoor lawn furniture only. Oversized grills allowed for personal use. Pets fine on leash in camping, parking areas.

Coos Bay Speedway

94320 Hwy. 42, Coos Bay, OR 97420

(541) 269-2474

coosbayspeedway.us

NHRA

Coos Bay accommodates more than 1,000 vehicles for camping, parking. Camping limited to weekends with races on Friday, Sunday. Other campgrounds within 20-minute drive. Parking, camping free. All personal vehicles fine. No tailgating furniture. Alcohol fine in camping areas, not in pits. Burning bans may prevent open fires. Keep pets on leash; stay in camping, parking areas.

Cordova Dragway Park

19425 IL Rt. 84 N., Cordova, IL 61242

(309) 654-2110

cordovadragwaypark.com

NHRA

Cordova has 5,000 day-parking spaces, 100 camping spaces. Special VIP parking next to track, $30–$100 per weekend. Otherwise, all parking, camping free. Restroom facilities with showers available. Personal vehicles allowed—except motorcycles. No glass allowed. Open fires okay; fire rings provided. Keep pets on leash; stay in camping areas. Park has climate-controlled café, game room, and playground.

Dakota Flat Track

2005 Burdict Expressway E., Minot, ND 58701

(701) 833-8465

dakotaflattrack.com

IHRA

Track has 8,000 day-parking spaces, 5,000 camping spaces—2,000 with hookups. Additional campgrounds across street; others within 20 minutes. Day parking free. Campsite with hookup $8 per day; dry camping free. Personal vehicles allowed. Open fires okay in portable fire pits. No alcohol brought into grandstands. Keep pets on leash; stay in camping area.

Darlington Dragway

2056 E. Bobo Newsom Hwy., Hartsville, SC 29550

(843) 383-0008

IHRA

Dragway has approximately 30 acres day parking. No overnight RV or tent camping. Shade canopies only; tailgating furniture allowed. Motorcycles allowed, if riders are 16 years or older and licensed; 15 mph speed limit; no bicycles or other personal vehicles. Alcohol okay; no glass. All admission tickets are also pit passes.

Darlington Raceway

1301 Harry Byrd Hwy., Darlington, SC 29532

(866) 459-7223

darlingtonraceway.com

Nextel Cup, Busch Series

Camping: Infield RV camping $475 for weekend with hookups, two admissions included. Other RV camping sites $100 per race week; no hookups. Family-oriented camping for vans, cars, pickups $300–$590 for weekend. Additional tent camping available for $75. Open fires contained in lined pit or fire ring allowed. Generators not allowed in infield. No pets. **Grandstand:** In grandstand, fans allowed one soft-sided, insulated cooler or bag, up to 6 x 6 x 12 inches, one clear plastic bag, up to 18 x 18 x 4 inches. No fireworks, hard-sided coolers, glass; no thermoses, insulated cups; no strollers, umbrellas.

Daytona International Speedway

1801 W. International Speedway Blvd., Daytona Beach, FL 32114

(386) 253-7223

daytonainternationalspeedway.com

Nextel Cup, Busch Series, Craftsman Trucks

Camping: RV camping prices $200–$2,750, includes 2 tickets. No hookups. Length of stay three to nine days, depending on event, ticket package. Each event has different pricing structure. Call for info. **Grandstand:** In grandstand, fans allowed one soft-sided cooler or bag, up to 6 x 6 x 12 inches, one clear plastic bag up to 18 x 18 x 4 inches. Seat cushions allowed. No hard-sided coolers, glass, thermos bottles, or insulated cups; no strollers, umbrellas, oversized bags, backpacks, or other containers. Note: Sit row 20 or higher in grandstand to see whole track.

Denton Dragway

Memory Lane, Denton, TX 76092 (off I-35 Exit 473)

(940) 482-6989

dentondragway.com

NHRA

Denton has over 2,000 parking spaces. Parking included in admission fee. Overnight parking allowed on race days—Friday and Saturday. Tailgating and day parking start at noon, finish 2 hours after end of race. Personal vehicles allowed in parking areas. Open fires allowed in approved fire pits. Keep pets leashed.

Desert Thunder Raceway

7400 Interstate Hwy. 20 W., Midland, TX 79706

(432) 687-2910

desertthunderraceway.com

IHRA

Raceway has more than 20 acres parking. Camping allowed for multiday race events. Camping area locked up overnight. Parking, camping free. Another campground 5 miles away. All personal vehicles must be licensed; speed limit 5 mph. Canopies, decorations can't obstruct view of track. Keep all furniture, equipment within confined camp space. No glass; BYOB alcohol. No open fires.

Dorchester Dragway

216 Delee Circle, Dorchester, SC 29437

(843) 563-5412 or (843) 563-1885

dorchesterdrag.com

IHRA

Dragway has 10 acres parking, camping. Day parking, camping free. Campers, tailgaters use outdoor furniture in site only. BYOB alcohol; no glass. Only small, 12- to 14-inch grills allowed. No open fires. Pets on leash fine; no large or aggressive breeds.

Dover International Speedway

1131 N. Dupont Hwy., Dover, DE 19901

(800) 441-RACE

doverspeedway.com

Nextel Cup, Busch Series, Craftsman Truck Series, NASCAR Regionals

Camping: No infield camping, but 3,500 RV sites available outside track. General RV camping $60 for event in Lots 7, 8, 9, 10; reserved camping runs $130–$200. Infield day parking available Sunday only, for $60. Other day parking free Friday, Saturday, but $10 on Sunday. Campground-to-track shuttles free; park-n-ride round trip shuttle available $10 from Christiana Mall, $20 from Blue Hen Corp. Center. In camping areas, keep flags, other decorations 100 feet from phone, power lines. Keep flags no higher than 5 feet above top of vehicle. No personal motorized vehicles; bikes okay. City ordinance prohibits tent camping. Observe quiet hours. **Grandstand:** In grandstand, fans allowed one cooler or bag up to 14 inches on all sides. Seat cushions, cameras, other personal electronics allowed. Call ahead for camcorders. No glass or alcohol; no strollers, umbrellas, or oversized bags; no pets; no fireworks or items posing safety or health risk.

Douglas County Speedway

2110 SW Frear St., Roseburg, OR 97470

(541) 440-4396

co.douglas.or.us/dcfair/index.html

NASCAR Regional

Speedway part of Douglas County Fairgrounds. Property covers 74 acres. Fifty camping sites available, with hookups. Campers allowed 14-day total stay, $20 per night with hookups, $15 without. Day parking free. Motorcycles, bikes allowed; no other personal vehicles. No tailgating furniture allowed. Cannot bring alcohol or have it in parking lot. No glass; no open fires.

Douglas Motorsports Park

1560 Lonnie Walker Rd., Nicholls, GA 31554

(912) 384-7733

douglasmotorsportspark.com

IHRA, NHRA

Park has 80 acres of parking, camping. No hard rules on camping arrival or departure times; use common sense. Day parking free; overnight camping $5. Personal vehicles allowed; open fires in designated areas only. No tailgating furniture or pets allowed. Alcohol fine, but BYOB since park doesn't sell it.

Dragway 42

9161 Rainbow Hwy., West Salem, OH 44287

(419) 853-4242

dragway42.com

IHRA

Dragway has 1,200 parking, camping spaces. Overnight camping allowed, but only for night of race—campers leave next morning. Parking, camping free. Six other campgrounds located within 20 minutes of track. Personal vehicles allowed; no glass. Pets on leash okay, limited to campgrounds.

Dubuque Fairgrounds Speedway

14583 Old Hwy. Rd., Dubuque, IA 52001

(563) 744-3620

simmonspromotionsinc.com

Dodge Weekly

Speedway has 3,000 day-parking spaces, 50 camping sites with hookups. Another campground located within 20 minutes. No hard rules on camping arrival or departure times; use common sense. Personal vehicles allowed, limited to parking, camping areas. Alcohol stays in camping, parking areas. Open fires allowed. Pets on leash okay, limited to campgrounds.

Dunn Benson Dragstrip

555 Dragstrip Rd., Benson, NC 27504

(919) 894-8502

dunnbensondragstrip.com

IHRA

Dragstrip has 11 acres for day parking. Overnight camping only during large events; 20 hookups available. Overnight stays limited to nights between two races. Parking, camping free. Personal vehicles allowed. No tailgating furniture or glass. BYOB alcohol; facility doesn't sell it. No pets.

Eddyville Raceway

3260 Merino Ave., Oskaloosa, IA 52577

(641) 969-5596

eddyvilleraceway.com

IHRA

Park has 60 acres for parking, camping; both free. No personal vehicles or tailgating furniture. BYOB alcohol; facility doesn't sell it. Open fires allowed, unless burning ban in effect. Note: Track under new ownership. Policies may change—call ahead.

Edgewater Sports Park

4819 E. Miami River Rd., Cleves, OH 45002

(513) 353-4666

edgewaterrace.com

NHRA

Park has 100 acres open space for parking, camping. Infield available during big events for overflow. Both parking, camping free. Camping limited to race weekend nights. Additional campgrounds available within 7 minutes of track. All personal vehicles allowed. No tailgating furniture or glass.

Edinburg International Racetrack

15920 N. Hwy. 281, Edinburg, TX 78541

(956) 318-0355

edinburgracetrack.com

IHRA

Racetrack has 6,000 parking spaces for camping, parking. Hookups at 25 sites. Camping free with purchase of weekend ticket. Day parking free. No motorized personal vehicles; bikes okay. BYOB alcohol; facility doesn't sell it. No glass or open fires. Nearby Echo Hotel offers discounts to spectators.

Elk Creek Dragway

711 Victory Lane, Elk Creek, VA 24326

(276) 228-7223

elkcreekdragway.com

IHRA

Dragway has 1,000 parking spaces, day use only. Parking fee included in admission price. Tailgating and parking start at noon, finish 1 hour after end of event. No glass allowed at track. No open fires or pets allowed.

Elko Speedway

26350 France Ave., Elko, MN 55020

(800) 479-3630

goelkospeedway.com

Dodge Weekly

Speedway has two open lots for parking. No camping or tailgating allowed. Overnight parking available, but not encouraged. One night only. All parking free.

Emerald Coast Dragway

7134 Garner Landing Rd., Holt, FL 32564

(850) 537-7223

emeraldcoastdragway.com

NHRA

Dragway has 500 parking spaces, plus 75 RV sites. RV size limit 30 feet. Parking, camping for NHRA events free. Personal vehicles okay. No alcohol allowed.

English Mountain Dragway

1325 Lewis Rd., Newport, TN 37821

(423) 625-8375

englishmountaindragway.com

IHRA

Dragway camping, parking in open field. Overnight camping on Friday, Saturday. Parking, camping free. Nearby campgrounds 4 miles away, in Gatlinburg. Personal vehicles okay. Don't ride bicycles during races. Keep alcohol in plain container.

ESTA Safety Park

8091 Eastwood Rd., Cicero, NY 13039

(315) 699-7484

estadrags.com

NHRA

Park has space for 400 vehicles. No overnight camping, parking. Sunday-only race day; arrive 7 a.m., leave by dark. Personal vehicles allowed for adults only. BYOB alcohol fine; no glass allowed. Keep open fires in fire ring. All admission tickets are all-access passes; children under 8 years free.

E.T. Raceway

RR 1, Lyons, IN 47443

(812) 384-4959

etraceway.com

NHRA

Raceway has more than 10 acres for parking, camping. Overnight camping allowed, limited to race weekend—must prearrange with management. Both camping, day parking free. All personal vehicles allowed. No tailgating furniture allowed. No glass. No dumping coals on grass; put cold coals in dump barrels provided. No open fires; no pets.

Evergreen Speedway

14405 179th Ave. SE, Monroe, WA 98272

(360) 805-6100

evergreenspeedway.net

NASCAR Regional, Dodge Weekly

Evergreen has 2,000 parking places, for day use only. Parking included in price of admission. Tailgating and parking start around 3:30 p.m., end 1 hour after race's conclusion. No glass, open fires, or pets allowed at track. All seats are general admission. Coolers and bags must fit under seats. Try to catch the school buses racing on a figure-eight course. It's pretty cool.

Farley Speedway

27317 Olde Farley Rd., Farley, IA 52046

(563) 744-3620

simmonspromotionsinc.com

Dodge Weekly

Speedway has 3,000 parking spaces; 50 RV sites have hookups. Parking, camping free. No set rule on arrival or departure times; use common sense. Additional campground within 20 minutes of track. Personal vehicles, alcohol, fine but limited to parking, camping areas. No oversized grills. Keep pets in camping area, on leash.

Farmington Motorsports Park
2992 Hwy. 801 N., Mocksville, NC 27028
(336) 998-3443
farmingtondragway.net
IHRA

Dragway has day parking for 10,000. Dry RV sites available with dump site. Pit area has additional 500 sites. Parking, camping free. No set rule on arrival, departure times, but campers need prior approval to stay longer than event weekend. Nearby campgrounds, Lake Meyers RV Resort, 15 minutes from track, Tanglewood Park 20 minutes. No bicycles; personal motorized vehicles okay. No tailgating furniture or glass. No open fires. Oversized grills okay; no selling food. Keep pets in camping area, on leash.

Fayetteville Motorsports Park
4480 Doc Bennet Rd., Fayetteville, NC 28306
(910) 484-3677
fayettevillemotorsportspark.com
IHRA

Park has 2,000 parking and camping spaces. Both included in admission fee. Campers can arrive a day early, stay overnight. Tailgating can start at sunrise race day; everyone must leave 1 hour after race ends. Open fires are fine if watched carefully. Keep personal vehicles in parking area. Keep any glass out in parking lot. First Friday of any month is "Freaky Friday" with that month's theme. Park is adjacent to Fayetteville Motorsports Speedway.

Firebird International Speedway

20,000 S. Maricopa Rd., Gate 2, Chandler, AZ 85226

(602) 268-0200

firebirdraceway.com

NHRA

Note that Speedway allows camping, tailgating during NHRA Checker Schucks Kragen Nationals only. Firebird has 20,000 day-parking spaces, 250 camping sites in Camp Firebird. No hookups; dumping station is available. Day parking $7. Camping runs $50–$75 for entire event. Trackside camping RVs only, runs $800; includes four three-day tickets. Continuous free shuttles available for handicapped. No personal motorized vehicles; bikes okay. No tents; no driving stakes into ground. Keep tailgating furniture within space. No furniture allowed at trackside RV spaces. No alcohol, pets, or open fires.

Firebird Raceway Park

8551 Hwy. 16, Eagle, ID 83616

(208) 938-8986

firebirdonline.com

NHRA

Park has 5,000 day-only parking spaces. Parking runs $5–$7 depending on event. No overnight camping or tailgating allowed at this facility. Out-of-town visitors should request Firebird rate at hotels within 5 miles of track. Raceway's theme is "A Track for All Reasons"—except for camping and tailgating, that is.

Gainesville Raceway

11211 N. County Rd. 225, Gainesville, FL 32609

(352) 377-0046

gainesvilleraceway.com

NHRA

Raceway has about 300 acres parking, camping. Camping allowed only during multiday events; campers stay overnight between race days, not before or after. RV, oversized vehicle size limit 60 feet. Most parking, camping free. During NHRA POWERade Series, campers pay $302.50 for six-day event. Shuttles available during POWERade Series. All personal vehicles fine. No camping tents, tailgating furniture, or open fires. Keep alcohol in parking, camping areas. Pets must be leashed or confined within RV. Burning bans may prevent use of grills; otherwise, grills fine.

Gateway International Speedway
700 Raceway Blvd., Madison, IL 62060
(866) 35-SPEED
gatewayraceway.com
Busch Series, Craftsman Truck Series

Gateway offers camping sites for NASCAR and NHRA events. If full, additional camping at Casino Queen and Horseshoe Lake. NASCAR camping $655 for season, includes four season tickets. NHRA camping $540 for weekend, plus two weekend tickets. Day parking $15 in advance, $20 day of event. Park-n-ride shuttle from Emerson Parkway Metro Link Station $5 round trip. In camping areas, no pets; no tent camping; no personal motorized vehicles, ground fires, hard liquor, or charcoal grills (gas grills okay). Beer in cans.

Grand Prix of Cleveland
Cleveland Burke Lakefront Airport (BKL)
1501 N. Marginal Dr., Cleveland, OH 44114
(216) 619-7223
grandprixofcleveland.com
Champ Car

Camping passes available in advance, $100 first-come, first-served for 3-day event. No hookups. Day parking $20 for 3-day pass. Single-day passes not available. City municipal lots $10 per day. Downtown metered parking free Saturdays and Sundays. On-site shuttles free, $1 from downtown one-way, or unlimited rides with $3 all-day pass. No personal motorized vehicles; bicycles okay. Only gas grills allowed; no charcoal. Grand Prix includes Family Zone, beer gardens, live music, exhibits, food and drink, go-kart racing, Miss Grand Prix of Cleveland contest.

Grand Prix of Denver Pepsi Center

1000 Chopper Circle, Denver, CO 80204
Tickets: (877) 77-CLICK
Information: (303) 825-0300
gpdenver.com
Champ Car

All parking downtown. Local city lots $6 and up ($7 is median) to park for day. Denver has excellent bus/public transit system. Light rail available; local unlimited all-day pass $4.50. Visit rtd-denver.com for more info. No tailgating, camping outside; all activities inside venue gates. Grand Prix has festival-like atmosphere, with concerts, motocross, a street party, plus more. In grandstand, fans allowed coolers up to 17 inches, all sides. No oversized coolers, alcohol, glass, stadium seats, oversized umbrellas, or lawn furniture. No bikes, skateboards, scooters, skates, or in-line skates; no ladders or step-stools; no banners.

Grand Prix of Houston

One Reliant Park, Houston, TX 77054
(713) 659-7223
grandprixofhouston.com
Champ Car

Grand Prix uses Reliant Park facility. Parking runs $10–$25, depending on location. Overnight parking allowed. Reliant staff did not provide further tailgating information. But for Houston Texans games (played at Reliant Stadium on the same property), the following rules apply: all RVs purchase two parking spots, park in designated RV areas. Tailgating limited to parking spot and space behind vehicle. No drinking alcohol Sundays before 10 a.m. Large balloons no longer permitted as decorations; all tents must be taken down before entering Grand Prix area.

Grand Prix of Long Beach

Long Beach Convention & Entertainment Center

300 E. Ocean Blvd., Long Beach, CA 90806

(888) 82-SPEED (827-7333)

longbeachgp.com

Champ Car

No camping, tailgating outside facility. About 1,000 spaces available for vehicles. Cars park on Marina or Shoreline Drive, $15 per day, or three-day parking pass $40–$50 depending on street. RVs park on Shoreline Drive only, same price as cars. Several bars, restaurants inside track; also Lifestyle Expo, Family Fun Zone, extreme sports demonstrations, other attractions.

Grand Prix of San Jose

300 Almaden Blvd., San Jose, CA 95110

(408) 277-9470

sanjosegrandprix.com

Champ Car

Grand Prix uses city parking garages; no space allotted for RVs or other motorcoaches. No camping, tailgating. Day parking $15 Saturday, Sunday during day; $5 Friday, Saturday evening 6 p.m. to 6 a.m.; free Sunday evening. Use city's bus, light-rail systems adjacent to distant lots, track. Light rail best bargain is 8-hour Excursion Pass, $3.50 per person. Best bus deal: one-way ride $1.75 per person. Inside facility, nonstop scheduled activities, including concerts. Cooler under 14 inches any side allowed. No pets allowed.

Grand Prix of St. Petersburg

Mahaffey Theatre/Bayfront Center

400 1st St. S., St. Petersburg, FL 33701

(727) 898-INDY (ext. 225)

gpstpete.com

IRL

Parking available throughout city; most day-trip fans park by Tropicana Field. Sixty dry RV spots available alongside start/finish line. RV spots $1,000 but include six general admission tickets and paddock passes for entire event. Day parking $7 at Tropicana Field, or park across from track for $20–$30. Shuttles run from Tropicana to racetrack. Nearby marina has space for up to 40 large yachts. No open fires. Leave coolers, stadium seats, etc., in vehicle.

Grandview Speedway

Passmore Rd., Bechtelsville, PA 19505

(610) 754-7688

grandviewspeedway.com

Dodge Weekly

Speedway has parking, camping for 1,000 vehicles; both free. Other campgrounds available ½ mile from track. All personal vehicles fine. Grills must be properly maintained; security inspects all grills. BYOB alcohol; facility doesn't sell it. No glass; remove all decorations, tailgating furniture when departing. Keep pets leashed or in RVs, away from track. Speedway has dirt track.

Great Lakes Dragway (Da Grove)

18411 1st St., Union Grove, WI 53182

(262) 878-3783

greatlakesdragaway.com

NHRA

Da Grove has more than 4,000 spaces for primitive overnight camping and day parking. All included in admission price. Management's pretty laid back—little is prohibited; just keep it all confined to parking, camping areas and don't go crazy. Da Grove has large, open field available for rent. Host your own private shebang.

Greenville Pickens Speedway
3800 Calhoun Memorial Hwy., Greenville, SC 29611
(864) 269-0852
greenvillepickens.com
NASCAR Regional, Dodge Weekly

Speedway has open-field parking. RV camping includes 30 sites with hookups, 500 dry sites in back stretch. No set rule on arrival, departure times; use common sense. Spaces with hookups $20 per night; other camping, day parking free. Personal vehicles fine; leave bikes in camping, parking areas. No tailgating furniture, glass, or open fires; no pets. Keep alcohol in plain container. Oversized grills fine for personal use only.

Greer Dragway
1792 Dragway Rd., Greer, SC 29651
(864) 877-0457
greerdragway.com
IHRA

Greer has 2,500 parking, camping spaces. Campsites dry, but dump station available. No set rules on arrival, departure times; use common sense. Non-campers arrive 3 hours before race, leave 1 hour after. All parking, camping free. No personal motorized vehicles; bikes okay for riders 16 years and up with driver's license. No tailgating furniture or glass. BYOB alcohol; keep in cups. Open fires okay, unless burning ban's in effect. Small pets on leashes okay; no large or aggressive breeds.

Grove Creek Raceway

55629 U.S. Hwy. 12, Grove City, MN 56243

(612) 280-7301

grovecreek.com

NHRA

Grove Creek has more than 500 parking, camping spaces. Overnight camping allowed only during race nights. Tailgaters arrive 2 hours before gates open, leave before next morning. Day parking free; camping $10 per night. Only motorcycles, bikes allowed as personal vehicles. Motorcycles must register with track, have valid license. No tailgating furniture or pets.

Heartland Park Topeka

7530 S. Topeka Blvd., Topeka, KS 66619

Office: (785) 862-4781

Tickets: (800) 43-RACES

hpt.com

NHRA

Heartland has 130 acres open parking, dry camping; 390 sites with full or partial hookups. Campers stay first to last night of event, not before or after. Parking, dry camping all free. Camping with hookups $50–$250 per event, depending on event, location. Personal vehicles allowed with purchase of $25 pit pass, except during NHRA events. Bikes always okay. No glass; open fires okay in rock ring if no burning ban in effect. Keep pets on leash, confined to camping area. Track located 4 miles south of Topeka Turnpike, Exit 177.

Hickory Motor Speedway

3130 Hwy. 70 SE, Newton, NC 28658

(828) 464-3655

hickorymotorspeedway.com

NASCAR Regional, Dodge Weekly

Speedway has more than 2,000 spaces for parking, camping. Additional 500 spaces track-side at Turns 3, 4. Camping available Friday through Monday noon. All parking, camping free, except trackside parking. Trackside first-come, first-served for $1. No glass; alcohol stays in parking, camping areas. Oversized grills, decorations for tailgate, campsite okay with speedway's permission.

Hilo Dragstrip

25 Aupuni St., Hilo, HI 96720

(808) 961-8697

islandracer.com

IHRA

Dragstrip has 10 acres day parking; no camping. Parking free. Tailgaters arrive as early as 7 a.m., leave by 8 p.m. No motorized personal vehicles, but bikes okay. No alcohol, tailgating furniture, or pets. No open fires. Dragstrip is county-owned land. Forestry land surrounds the track. Distance from gate to track is about 3 miles.

Hobbs Motorsports Park

5333 N. A St., Hobbs, NM 88240

(505) 391-8283

hobbsmotorsportspark.com

NHRA

Park ½ mile along track fence; watch race from vehicle. Overnight stays during multiday events only; no hookups. Parking, camping free. State park campground ½ mile away with full hookups. Personal vehicles must be licensed. No alcohol or open fires. Grills must be off ground. Casino nearby; try your luck.

Holland International Speedway

11586 Holland Glenwood Rd., Holland, NY 14080

(716) 537-2272

hollandspeedway.com

NASCAR Regional, Dodge Weekly

All parking, camping in open field. No set rules for camper arrival, departure times; use common sense. Parking, camping free. Other nearby campgrounds within 5 miles. All personal vehicles fine, except ATVs. Alcohol stays in parking, camping area.

Holly Springs Motorsports

159 Old Hwy. 7 S., Holly Springs, MS 38635

(662) 252-5600 (weekends only)

NHRA

Holly Springs has 1,000 day-parking spaces; no overnight camping. Parking free. No personal vehicles, except bicycles. No alcohol, tailgating furniture, or grills. No glass or open fires.

Homestead-Miami Speedway

1 Speedway Blvd., Homestead, FL 33035

(305) 230-7223

homesteadmiamispeedway.com

Nextel Cup, Busch Series, Craftsman Trucks

Camping: RV camping $250 for weekend, tickets not included. No infield camping. Day parking free. In camping areas, no bikes, personal motorized vehicles, or open fires. No metal flag poles; no flags higher than 15 feet. Poles must be more than 20 feet from phone, power lines. No tractor trailers, lift trucks, or box trucks. No platforms or scaffolding. Campgrounds patrolled by law enforcement. **Grandstand:** In grandstand, fans allowed one soft-sided bag or cooler up to 6 x 6 x 12 inches, one plastic bag up to 18 x 18 x 4 inches. Camcorders, other personal electronics allowed. No glass, oversized bags, or hard-sided coolers; no strollers, chairs, or umbrellas; no wagons, bicycles, Rollerblades, or skateboards.

Houston Motorsports Park

11620 N. Lake Houston Pkwy., Houston, TX 77044

(281) 458-1972

houstonmotorsportspark.com

NHRA

This track did not provide additional information about tailgating or race-day regulations.

Houston Raceway Park

2525 FM 565, Baytown, TX 77522

(281) 383-7223 (RACE)

houstonraceway.com

NHRA

Park has large area for parking, camping, both usually free. Track staff was unable to provide further details.

Hub City Dragway

331 Eatonville Rd., Hattiesburg, MS 39401

(601) 545-3724

hubcitydragway.com

IHRA

Dragway has 2,000 parking places, day use only. Parking included in admission fee. Tailgating and day parking start at noon, wrap up 1 hour after end of race. No overnight parking. No tailgating furniture, shade canopies, or personal vehicles allowed. Pets must be leashed. Hub City's Café now open.

Huntsville Dragway

502 Quarter Mountain Rd., Harvest, AL 35749

Weekday: (205) 251-7311

Recording: (256) 859-0807

huntsvilledragway.com

NHRA

Dragway has more than 1,000 day-parking spaces, all free. No camping or tailgating allowed. Personal vehicles allowed.

I-40 Dragway

1650 Creston Rd., Crossville, TN 38571

(931) 456-1584

i40dragway.com

IHRA

Dragway has up to 500 spaces available for parking, camping. Overnight camping only during large events, for nights between races. No personal vehicles; no shade canopies, tailgating furniture, or alcohol; no glass decorations or open fires. Only small grills allowed.

I-80 Speedway at Nebraska Raceway Park

I-80 Exit #420 Greenwood, NE 68366

(402) 342-3453

neracewaypark.com

Dodge Weekly

Speedway has 50 acres open parking, camping, both free. No set rules for arrival or departure times; use common sense. No glass allowed. Remove all tailgating, camping items upon departure.

I-94 Raceway

410th St., Sauk Centre, MN 56378

(320) 352-5263

i94raceway.com

NASCAR Regional

Raceway has 2,000 parking spaces, with overnight camping allowed on race days only. Parking is $30 for RVs, $20 for cars. Open fires must be contained in a fire pit. All pets must be leashed. Tailgating and day parking start at 5:30 p.m. and end 1 hour after conclusion of race.

Immokalee Regional Raceway

State Rd. 846 E., Immokalee, FL 34142

(239) 657-5954

immrace.com

IHRA

Raceway has 2,000 parking spaces for camping, parking. Camping available during event nights only. No personal vehicles, shade canopies, camping tents, or tailgating furniture. No alcohol or open fires.

Indianapolis Motor Speedway

4790 W. 16th St., Indianapolis, IN 46222

(800) 822-4639

indianapolismotorspeedway.com

Nextel Cup, IRL

Camping: RVs camp in eight lots, but not infield. Infield day parking available for cars, trucks, vans only. Camping for four days runs $120–$250, depending on lot. RV or bus day parking $40. For cars, day parking $20 per day for Nextel, $30 for Indy 500, or three-day weekend pass $40. Tailgating for day parking allowed inside Turn 3, Turn 1, and Lots 1B, 1C, 2, 3, 7. In campgrounds, keep flag poles 50 feet away from power lines. Tent camping in Lots 4, 1A, 1C. No personal motorized vehicles except motorcycles, mopeds ridden to and from street to campsite. Canopies up to 10 x 10 feet okay; take down before green flag. No scaffolds, platforms, or box trucks. Lots 4 and 6 family-friendly. No dumping of charcoal or ashes. RVs leave at end of event, not next day. **Grandstand:** In grandstand, fans allowed one cooler or bag up to 14 inches every side; small backpacks, bag for food and personal items allowed. Camcorders, other personal electronics allowed. No over-sized bags, fireworks, flares, or glass; no strollers, lawn chairs, or folding camp chairs; no Rollerblades, skateboards, skates, scooters, bicycles, or items posing safety threat.

Infineon Raceway

Hwy. 37 & Hwy. 121, Sonoma, CA 95476
(800) 870-RACE
infineonraceway.com
Nextel Cup, NASCAR Regional, IRL, NHRA

Camping: More than 1,400 RV camping spaces for Nextel events, $54.50–$1,584.60, depending on site and event. Day parking free. In campgrounds no open fires, glass, motorized vehicles, offensive signs, public drunkenness, or profanity. No selling alcohol to other campers. RV pump services available at NASCAR, NHRA, IRL events. Bring what you need—closest store 15 miles away. **Grandstand:** In grandstand, fans allowed one cooler and bags/backpacks up to 15 inches all sides; plastic bottles, seat cushions, stadium seats allowed. Camcorders, other personal electronic devices also allowed. No alcohol, cans, or glass; no lawn chairs or umbrellas allowed. Child wristbands are available.

Interstate Dragways

4147 70th St. S. (CR-11), Glyndon, MN 56547
(218) 236-9461
interstatedragways.com
NHRA

Interstate has 2,000 parking spaces available. Overnight camping permitted on event days only, Friday through Sunday. Parking included in admission fee. Spectators can park cars or start tailgating anytime during race days; just quit when you're tired. No personal vehicles, shade canopies, tents, or tailgating furniture allowed in parking areas. Open fires allowed in contained pits. Pets must be leashed.

Iron Springs Speedway

9205 W. Antelope Springs Rd., Cedar City, UT 84720

(435) 559-8416

ironspringsspeedway.com

IHRA

Speedway has more than 20 acres day parking, 30 camping spots with full hookups. Camping available for nights of weekend events only. Day parking free; camping $30 per night with hookups, $10 without. Personal vehicles obey 5 mph speed limit. Leave camping, tailgating area clean when departing. No glass or open fires. BYOB alcohol; facility doesn't sell.

Irwindale Dragstrip

500 Speedway Dr., Irwindale, CA 91706

(626) 358-1100

irwindalespeedway.com /dragstrip/index.asp

NHRA

Irwindale has 3,000 vehicle spaces. No camping at dragstrip. All parking free. Licensed motorcycles are only personal vehicles allowed. Grills are okay; no tents, tailgating furniture, or alcohol allowed. No pets or open fires. Four Points Hotel gives spectators discounts. Check Web site for details.

Irwindale Speedway

500 Speedway Dr., Irwindale, CA 91706

(626) 358-1100

irwindalespeedway.com

NASCAR Regional, Dodge Weekly

Speedway, dragstrip share same location. Irwindale has 3,000 spaces for parking, camping. Camping allowed at oval track for event nights only. Parking, camping both $5. Licensed motorcycles are only personal vehicles allowed. Grills okay; no tents, tailgating furniture, or alcohol allowed. No pets or open fires. Four Points Hotel gives spectators discounts. Check Web site for details.

Island Dragway

20 Island Rd., Great Meadows, NJ 07838

(908) 637-6060

islanddragway.com

NHRA

Dragway has 300 parking spaces, no overnight camping. Parking free. No personal vehicles, alcohol, or open fires. Grills allowed at regular events, not special events. Bring bug spray.

Jackson Dragway Park

7557 Siwell Rd., Byram, MS 39272

(601) 372-5506

jxndragway.com

NHRA

Park has 10 acres day parking, no overnight camping. RV campground ½ mile from track. No personal vehicles, alcohol, or grills. No tailgating furniture, glass, or pets.

Jefferson-Pageland Dragway

3167 Peach Orchard Rd., Jefferson, SC 29718

(704) 821-7355

jeffersonpagelanddragway.com

IHRA

Dragway has 50 acres open parking, camping. Camping during major events only. If camping, arriving night before race allowed. All leave at end of event. All parking, camping free. No open fires; no glass. BYOB alcohol; dragway doesn't sell.

Jennerstown Speedway

224 Race St., Jennerstown, PA 15547

(814) 629-6677

jennerstown.com

NASCAR Regional, Dodge Weekly

Speedway has more than 2,000 spaces for parking, camping. Camping allowed only during touring series events. Parking, camping free. Other campgrounds within 20 minutes of track. When camping's available, campers arrive night before event. No glass allowed. Keep food and drink in parking, camping area. Contained campfires permitted.

Julesburg Dragstrip

17454 Hwy. 138, Julesburg, CO 80737

(970) 463-0923

julesburgdragstrip.com

NHRA

Dragstrip has 100 total parking, camping spaces, all free. No set rules for campers, tailgaters on arrival, departure times; use best judgment. Personal vehicles fine in camping, parking area, not in pits. Alcohol fine, before or after race—not during. No open fires.

Kalamazoo Speedway

7656 Ravine Rd., Kalamazoo, MI 49009

(269) 692-2423

kalamazoospeedway.com

Dodge Weekly

Speedway offers 2,100 parking, camping spots, all free. No set rules for campers on arrival, departure times; use best judgment. Tailgaters arrive 9 a.m. Motorcycles, bikes allowed; no other personal vehicles. No glass. Security, first aid provided for larger events.

Kanawha Valley Motorsports Park

2319 State Rt. 35, Southside, WV 25187

(304) 675-6767

kanrace.com

IHRA

Kanawha has 7,000 multiuse parking spaces, all free. Camping available on race weekends, Thursday through Saturday. Nearby campgrounds 14 miles from track. No personal vehicles, tailgating furniture, or grills. No alcohol, glass, or open fires. No decorations. Security provided for bigger events.

Kansas City International Raceway

8201 Noland Rd., Kansas City, MO 64138

(816) 358-6700

kcir.net

NHRA

Raceway has more than 50 acres for camping, parking. Camping on big race weekends only, Friday to Sunday. Parking, camping both $5 per day; larger events may charge more. Nearby campground 5–10 miles from track. All personal vehicles allowed with $5 permit fee; must provide proof of insurance. Mini-motorcycles not allowed. Tents allowed on camping weekends. Raceway sells alcohol; don't BYOB. No open fires.

Kansas Speedway

400 Speedway Blvd., Kansas City, KS 66111

(866) 460-RACE (7223)

kansasspeedway.com

Nextel Cup, Busch Series, Craftsman Trucks, IRL

Camping: Speedway offers over 1,200 camping sites. Both sites and tickets sold by season only. Day parking free for cars, oversized vehicles in 65,000 spaces. In camping areas, no personal motorized vehicles, glass, open fires, or pets (boarding facilities nearby) allowed. No tent camping allowed. If sold out, speedway recommends nearby Cottonwood Campground, Bonner Springs, and The Woodlands camping areas. During race, keep flags below vehicle height. **Grandstand:** In grandstand, one 6 x 6 x 12 bag per person. No coolers, oversized bags, glass, alcohol, umbrellas, folding chairs, strollers, bicycles, wagons, scooters, Rollerblades, spray fans holding liquid, or outside food and beverages in grandstand. Ticket scalping illegal. Food, clothing, and convenience stores across road from speedway. Speedway has superior sightlines; entire track can be seen from all seats.

Kauai Raceway Park

Kaumualii Hwy. at Lighthouse Rd., Kekaha, HI 96752

(808) 823-6749

islandracer.com

NHRA

A tear-down track put up on state-owned property; 400 free parking spots. No overnight camping. Spectators arrive at noon, leave by 1 a.m. No personal vehicles or open fires. Alcohol fine, but not pit-side. No bleachers—tailgating the only way to go.

Kearney Raceway Park

4860 Imperial Ave., Kearney, NE 68847

(308) 832-0302

krpi.com

NHRA

Park has 250 all-purpose free parking spots. Camping only on nights between consecutive race days. Camping tents okay then. No personal vehicles. No alcohol or glass; no open fires or pets.

Kentucky Speedway

5120 Sparta Pike, Sparta, KY 41086

(859) 647-4309

kentuckyspeedway.com

Busch Series, Craftsman Truck, IRL

Camping starts at $30 first-come, first-served to $500 reserved. Day parking free for cars; buses pay $100. RVs can't park in day parking. No infield camping at speedway; Web site has list of nearby campgrounds. In campground, no glass, motorized vehicles; bikes okay. Fires in approved fire ring okay. Pets allowed in some camping areas; policy could change—call ahead. Keep everything within campsite.

Kil-Kare Dragway

1166 Dayton-Xenia Rd., Xenia, OH 45385

(937) 429-2961

kilkarespeedway.com

NHRA

This track did not provide additional information about tailgating or race-day regulations.

Kil-Kare Speedway

1166 Dayton-Xenia Rd., Xenia, OH 45385

(937) 429-2961

kilkarespeedway.com

Dodge Weekly

This track did not provide additional information about tailgating or race-day regulations.

Kinston Dragstrip

Hwy. 11 S., Kinston, NC 28504

(252) 522-9551

kdsmotorsports.com

IHRA

Strip has 1,500 all-purpose free parking spaces. Camping during two-day events only, night between race days only. Camping also free. Additional camping at lake behind dragstrip. Personal vehicles okay. Canopies, tents okay by lake area. No tailgating furniture at dragstrip. No glass or open fires; no rowdy behavior.

Knoxville Dragway

160 Raceway Dr., Maynardville, TN 37806

(865) 256-3112

knoxdragway.com

IHRA

Dragway has 18 acres free multiuse parking, camping. Camping okay only overnight between races. Additional campgrounds within 20 minutes of track. No personal vehicles, alcohol, or open fires. Pets allowed Saturdays only. Plainclothes security mixes with spectators during events.

LaCrosse Fairgrounds Speedway

N4985 County Hwy. M, West Salem, WI 54669

(608) 786-1525

lacrossespeedway.com

NASCAR Regional, Dodge Weekly

Speedway has 34 acres free multiuse parking, camping. Campers can stay up to one week. Camping free at fairgrounds except for Fair Week, mid-July. No personal vehicles. Open fires allowed in provided fire rings.

LaGrange Speedway

123 Heard Rd., LaGrange, GA 30240

(706) 302-3276 or (706) 302-1317

troupcountydrag.com

IHRA

Speedway can accommodate up to 400 cars, 75 RVs (no hookups or showers). All parking, camping free. Additional campgrounds within 15 minutes of track. Tailgaters arrive early as noon, leave by midnight. All personal vehicles allowed. No bicycles in staging lanes. People with oversized grills, smokers automatically charged vendor fee. BYOB alcohol; track doesn't sell it. No pets allowed.

Lake Erie Speedway

10700 Delmas Dr., North East, PA 16428

(814) 725-3303

lakeeriespeedway.com

NASCAR Regional, Dodge Weekly

Speedway has more than 2,000 all-purpose free parking spaces, plus overflow lot. Tailgaters come 2 hours before race, leave 1 hour after; no set rules for campers on arrival or departure. RVs should park in back of lot, away from traffic. Alcohol limited to camping, parking areas.

Lakeside Speedway

5615 Wolcott Dr., Kansas City, KS 66109

(913) 299-2040

lakesidespeedway.net

Dodge Weekly

Speedway has 20 acres open, all-purpose free parking, including large picnic area for tailgaters. Tailgaters arrive at 2 p.m.; otherwise, no set time limits for campers, tailgaters. Personal vehicles, alcohol both stay in parking area. Site should be clean, bare when departing. Speedway has charcoal, portable fire pits—first-come, first-served. (Open fires in portable fire pits only.)

Lakeview Dragstrip

Airport Rd., Lakeview, OR 97630

(541) 947-3970

na-motorsports.com/Tracks/OR/Lakeview.html

NHRA

Dragstrip has 80 free multiuse parking spaces. Camping allowed during weekend race nights only. Tailgaters arrive 9 a.m., leave 1 hour after race ends. No motorized personal vehicles; bikes okay. No tailgating furniture or open fires. No alcohol in pit area. Take decorations with you when leaving.

Lancaster Motorsports Park

57 Gunnville Rd., Lancaster, NY 14086

(716) 759-6818

lancasterracing.com

IHRA

Park has 5 acres free multiuse parking. No set rules for arrival, departure times for campers, tailgaters; use best judgment. All personal vehicles fine. Keep alcohol in parking areas. No pets allowed. Park runs 100 events per year on three separate tracks.

Langley Speedway

11 Dale Lemonds Dr., Hampton, VA 23666

(757) 865-7223

langley-speedway.com

Dodge Weekly

Speedway has 2,000 free day-parking spaces. No overnight camping; most parking spots too small to tailgate. Facility does have 10 RV parking spaces in Turns 3 and 4, just for tailgating; available to any type vehicle for $30. Other campgrounds at Newport News, 20 minutes from track. No personal vehicles, canopies, or tents. No tailgating furniture, grills, or open fires. No glass or hard liquor—beer only. No pets allowed.

Lanier National Speedway

One Raceway Dr., Braselton, GA 30517

(770) 967-8600

lanierspeedway.com

Dodge Weekly

Speedway has free terraced parking spaces, accommodating more than 2,500 guests. No camping during regular events; during big events, travelers can park RVs overnight. Limit one night. Spectators arrive 5 p.m., leave midnight. Motorcycles, bikes, golf carts are only personal vehicles allowed. Decorations okay, if not blocking view of track. Canopies or tents allowed on upper terraces, not trackside. No tailgating furniture or glass allowed. Alcohol, grilling limited to trackside area. No gas grills. Open fires allowed during major events.

Las Vegas Motor Speedway

7000 Las Vegas Blvd. N., Las Vegas, NV 89115

(800) 644-4444

lvms.com

Nextel Cup, Busch Series, Craftsman Trucks

Camping: Speedway has 1,400 acres parking, 4,500 RV camping sites. Day parking free; weekend parking passes available. RV camping runs $120–$3,000, depending on site and event. Infield under construction—no infield camping for 2007. If speedway camping sold out, Sam's Town Hotel & Casino, Silverton Hotel & Casino, Circus-Circus Resort & Casino have RV parks. In camping areas, no fires, motorized vehicles (bikes okay), external TVs, external sound systems, or glass. Keep flags away from power lines. No kites allowed due to low-flying planes. No box trucks, cargo trucks, rental trucks, or enclosed hauling trailers permitted. No tents or scaffolds. **Grandstand:** In grandstand, bottled water, camcorders, other personal electronics allowed. No coolers, umbrellas, or chairs; no outside food or drinks; no glass; no scaffolds; no noisemakers or horns; no helium balloons or beach balls. Security very tight.

Lebanon Valley Dragway

1746 U.S. Rt. 20, West Lebanon, NY 12195

(518) 794-7130

dragway.com

NHRA

Spectators, campers park in free grass lot across the street from dragway. No set time for spectators, campers to arrive or depart. Additional campgrounds 10 miles from track. Motorcycles, bikes are only personal vehicles allowed. Open fires must be contained. Pets stay in parking area. Alcohol in parking area only—keep it discreet; have ticket handy to show security. No glass.

Lee USA Speedway

280 Calef Hwy. (Rt. 125), Lee, NH 03824

(978) 462-4252

leeusaspeedway.com

Dodge Weekly

Speedway has up to 2,000 free, all-purpose parking spots. No motorized personal vehicles; bikes okay. No tailgating furniture, alcohol, or open fires. No pets allowed. Decorations encouraged.

Lewistown Raceway

Cottonwood Creek Rd., Lewistown, MT 59457

(406) 453-7555

lewistowndragracing.com

NHRA

This track did not provide additional information about tailgating or race-day regulations. Raceway is located on an inactive taxiway at the Lewistown Municipal Airport.

Lime Rock Park

497 Lime Rock Rd., Lakeville, CT 06039

(800) 722-3577

limerock.com

NASCAR Regional

Park has open lot for parking. All camping in infield. Both free with event ticket. For larger events, RV spots may be purchased in advance. Depending on event, prices run $100–$150 for full event. RV size limit under 10 tons (20,000 lbs), under 40 feet long, 12 feet wide. Park rents golf carts; bikes allowed in camping area. No other personal vehicles. No oversized grills or glass. Cooking in camping area only. Pets allowed on leash, but not encouraged. No grandstands—fans sit amphitheater style; bring blankets, chairs.

Linn County Speedway

Intersection of Hwy. 69 and 52 W., Pleasanton, KS 66075

(913) 352-6999

linncountyspeedway.com

Dodge Weekly

Speedway has 3,000 parking spaces, for day use only. Parking fees included in admission price. Tailgating, day parking start 2 hours before the race, end 1 hour afterward. No personal vehicles allowed. No tailgating furniture or shade canopies allowed. Open fires permitted in fire pits. Pets must be leashed. No outside food or beverages allowed inside gates.

London Dragway

3835 White Oak Rd., London, KY 40741
(606) 878-8883
londondragway.com
NHRA

Dragway has 2,000 day-use parking spaces and is located on the outskirts of Daniel Boone National Forest. Dragway doesn't allow overnight parking. Day parking and tailgating start at noon on race day, end 1 hour after conclusion of race. No personal vehicles allowed in parking areas. No tailgating furniture or shade canopies allowed. Open fires must be contained in fire pits. Keep pets leashed.

Lone Star Motorsports Park

120 Old Columbus Rd. S., Sealey, TX 77474
(713) 466-3420
lonestarmotorsportspark.com
IHRA

Lone Star has more than 100 acres free all-purpose parking. Personal vehicles all fine. No tailgating furniture, glass, or open fires; no pets. Motocross, road course recently added.

Los Angeles County Raceway

6850 E. Ave. T, Palmdale, CA 93550

(661) 533-2224

lacr.net

NHRA

Raceway has 250 multiuse parking spaces. Camping allowed during multiday events only, $10 for entire event. Day parking free. Personal vehicles fine; driver must be 18 years or older. Decorations must be affixed to vehicle. Take all tailgating furniture with you when leaving.

Lost Creek Raceway

Galen Rd., Anaconda, MT 59711

(406) 949-3724

lostcreek-raceway.com

NHRA

Raceway has 40 acres for parking. Campers may arrive the day before, leave the day after race day. Day parking included in admission fees. Call management about fees for overnight camping. Tailgating and day parking start as early as sunrise, end 1 hour after race's conclusion. Open fires not allowed; glass not permitted anywhere on property. Pets must be leashed.

Lowcountry Dragway

1209 Cypress Gardens Rd., Moncks Corner, SC 29461

(843) 761-2566

lowcountrydragway.com

IHRA

Dragway has 1,000 free parking spaces. No camping. Tailgaters arrive 2 hours before race, leave by midnight. All personal vehicles okay. No tailgating furniture or glass; BYOB alcohol. No open fires; keep pets on leash. Fenced-in playground for children.

Lowes Motor Speedway

5555 Concord Pkwy. S., Concord, NC 28027

(800) 455-FANS

lowesmotorspeedway.com

Nextel Cup, Busch Series, Craftsman Trucks

Camping: Lowes offers 7,000 camping sites, with 200 infield spaces. If sold out, three nearby campgrounds can assist. Day parking is free for cars, buses; RVs not allowed in day spaces. Camping fees run $70–$525 with full hookups available at Fleetwood RV Camping Resort. In campground area, no open fires, motorized vehicles, or bicycles allowed. Small pets allowed, if leashed. **Grandstand:** In grandstand, fans allowed coolers and bags up to 14 inches all sides; beverages in cans, camcorders, and other personal electronics allowed. No umbrellas, glass bottles, or strollers; no oversized bags, backpacks, or coolers; no stadium seats with arms; no skateboards, roller skates, scooters, bicycles, motorized vehicles; no beach balls, balloons; no signs, banners, or noisemakers.

Lubbock Dragway

9902 E. CR 6300, Idalou, TX 79329

(806) 762-0627

lubbockdragway.com

NHRA

Dragway has 1,000 multiuse free parking spaces. Overnight camping on race nights only. Additional campground 15 miles from track. All personal vehicles okay. No tailgating furniture or open fires. BYOB alcohol; no kegs allowed. Dragway in dry county.

Madras Dragstrip

NW Glass Dr., Madras, OR 97741

(541) 815-2107

madrasdragstrip.com

NHRA

Dragstrip has 5 acres all-purpose free parking. Camping on race weekends only, Friday through Sunday. Additional campground next to fairgrounds; another just outside town. Motorized personal vehicles okay; no bicycles. BYOB alcohol. Grills fine, extinguish coals with water. Keep decorations secure. Open fires okay; use rocks to contain. High winds require caution. No flush toilets. Leave site clean; dispose of trash off-site.

Magic Valley Speedway
3659 Grandview Dr. S., Twin Falls, ID 83301
(208) 734-3700
magicvalleyspeedway.com
NASCAR Regional, Dodge Weekly

Speedway has 1,000 free, multiuse spaces in gravel lot. Campers stay one night only. Three more campgrounds within 8 miles. Personal vehicles, alcohol restricted to gravel lot. Keep furniture, grills, etc., within spot. No glass, pets, or open fires.

Mansfield Motorsports Speedway
100 Crall Rd., Mansfield, OH 44903
(800) 424-0688
mansfield-speedway.com
Craftsman Trucks, Dodge Weekly, IHRA

Speedway has 50 acres for camping, space for 10,000 cars. RV or tent camping $50 for weekend during Craftsman Truck races; otherwise, camping free. Day parking for cars, oversized vehicles free. In camping areas, four-wheelers, golf carts allowed with permit only; bikes allowed. Open fires allowed in fire rings; must be 15 feet from camper. Drugstore and convenience store nearby.

Maple Grove Raceway

30 Stauffer Park Lane, Mohnton, PA 19540

(610) 856-7200

maplegroveraceway.com

NHRA

Raceway covers 517 acres of property. No camping—Maple Grove Park Campground ½ mile away; contact info on Web site. Spectators arrive 8 a.m., leave 1 hour after race. National event parking $10 for all vehicles; otherwise, free. Shuttles available at national events only. No personal vehicles, shade canopies, or tailgating furniture. No alcohol, grills, or open fires. Pets require signed waiver; must be leashed.

Marion County International Speedway

2303 Richwood LaRue Rd., LaRue, OH 43332

(740) 499-3666

mcir.com

IHRA

Raceway has 1,000 parking spaces, no camping. Use Hickory Grove Campground 14 miles away. No personal vehicles, tailgating furniture, or alcohol. Open fires only in fire ring, not on grass.

Martinsville Speedway

340 Speedway Rd., Martinsville, VA 24112

(877) RACE-TIX (722-3849)

martinsvillespeedway.com

Nextel Cup, Busch Series, Craftsman Trucks, NASCAR Regional

Camping: Martinsville has 250 acres for parking and camping. Infield camping not available. General RV camping prices $60 for event; reserved spaces run $250–$300 per year, or $100 per Nextel event. Tent camping is $20. In camping areas, wood fires allowed if above ground in fire ring. **Grandstand:** In grandstand, one soft-sided cooler *or* bag up to 6 x 6 x 12 inches allowed per person. One clear plastic bag, up to18 x 18 x 4 inches, per guest allowed. Seat cushions, binoculars, personal electronics allowed. No hard-sided coolers, thermos, or insulated cups; no strollers, umbrellas, or items restricted by track policy; no oversized bags, backpacks, or containers. Children's wristbands available. Note: Camping areas overlook track.

Maryland International Raceway

27861 Budds Creek Rd., Mechanicsville, MD 20659
(301) 884-DRAG
mirdrag.com
IHRA

Raceway management stresses all tailgating, camping regulations change with each event. All visitors urged to check Web site or information line for current event guidelines.

Mason Dixon Dragway

21003 National Pike, Boonsboro, MD 21713
(301) 791-5193
NHRA

Dragway has 3,000 spaces for parking. Overnight camping allowed during event days only. Parking included in admission fee. Tailgating and day parking start 2 hours before the race, end 1 hour afterward. Alcohol is allowed, but not kegs. Open fires allowed in fire pits. Glass not allowed. Keep pets leashed at all times.

Maui Raceway Park

Mokulele Hwy. at Mehameha Loop, Kihei, HI 96753

(808) 281-1273

mrp.org

NHRA

Park has 200 free day-parking spaces in lot, plus 100 more trackside. Personal vehicles allowed, except in pits. Drivers must be 18 years or older.

Memphis Motorsports Park

5500 Victory Lane, Memphis, TN 38053

(866) 40 SPEED

memphismotorsports.com

Busch Series, Craftsman Trucks, NHRA

Speedway offers 400 camping sites, 4,000 day-parking spaces. Camping for NASCAR events runs $25 per day to $60 for weekend. Camping for NHRA Nationals weekend either $99 (includes four general admission grandstand tickets) for nontrackside sites or $640 (no tickets) for sites along track's finish line. Day parking free for NASCAR events; $5 per day for NHRA Nationals. Memphis officials recommend avoiding private lots. In camping areas, no motorized vehicles or bicycles. Canopies must fit within 10 x 10-foot space. No corporate signage or banners. No oversized grills; elevated fire rings allowed for open fires. Track may remove external TVs or stereo systems if offensive or disruptive.

Meridian Speedway

335 E. 1st St. S., Meridian, ID 83642

(208) 888-2813

meridianspeedway.com

NASCAR Regional

This track did not provide additional information about tailgating or race-day regulations.

Michigan International Speedway

12626 U.S. Hwy. 12, Brooklyn, MI 49230-9068

(800) 354-1010

mispeedway.com

Nextel Cup, Busch Series, Craftsman Trucks, IRL

Camping: MIS offers enough parking for 40,000 vehicles. RV campers' arrival times vary from one to six days before event, depending on campground. Camping runs $75–$400, depending on event and campsite. Day-parking area free. In camping area, bicycles with reflectors okay. No motorized vehicles; no open fires; no glass; no pets—boarding area nearby. No super soakers, water balloon launchers, spotlights, laser pointers, or other items posing safety risk allowed. No semi-trailers or rental trucks. No offensive signs, drunkenness, or profanity. In day-parking areas, put away all tailgating equipment before entering grandstands. Environmental Notice: Due to Emerald Ash Borer infestation, Michigan prohibits transport of all hardwood firewood out of Lower Peninsula area. Buy wood locally, burn all on-site, or leave behind. Over 20 million ash trees in region killed by Ash Borer beetle. **Grandstand:** In grandstand, one soft-sided cooler or bag, up to 6 x 6 x 12 inches allowed per person; seat cushions, stadium seats okay; binoculars, personal electronics allowed. No hard-sided coolers, oversized bags; no glass; no umbrellas; no fireworks; no banners, flags; no strollers, ladders, bicycles, Rollerblades, or items posing safety risk.

Mid-America Dragway

Hwy. 166, Arkansas City, KS 67005

(620) 442-5350

midstatedragway.com

NHRA

This track did not provide additional information about tailgating or race-day regulations.

Mid-Michigan Motorplex

2589 N. Wyman Rd., Stanton, MI 48888

(989) 762-5043

midmichmotorplex.com

NHRA

Motorplex has 20 acres free day parking, 100 acres camping outside facility gates. No tent camping. Motorcycles, mopeds allowed if driven by licensed operator. Other personal vehicles prohibited. Open fires allowed in fire pits.

Midstate Dragway

12016 N. Cr-1650E, Havana, IL 62644

(217) 245-1776

midstatedragway.com

NHRA

This track did not provide additional information about tailgating or race-day regulations.

Milan Dragway

10860 Plank Rd., Milan, MI 48160

(734) 439-7368

milandragway.com

IHRA

Dragway has 1,000 spaces available. No camping. Parking runs $5–$10 for both RVs, cars. Season pass available for $100. Motorized personal vehicles okay. No glass allowed.

Milwaukee Mile
Wisconsin State Fairgrounds
601 S. 76th St., West Dallis, WI 53214
(414) 266-7035
milwaukeemile.com
Nextel Cup, Busch Series, Craftsman Trucks, IRL, Champ Car

Camping: All Milwaukee Mile parking at State Fairgrounds, 4,000 day-parking spaces. During NASCAR events, 600 RV camping spaces available, all capable of electric hookups, 70 with full hookups. Cost $40–$50 per night, depending on full or partial hookups. Minimum two- or three-night stay required, depending on event. Campers may arrive day before race. If daytime race, campers leave 1 hour after event; if evening race, campers stay overnight, leave in morning. General parking $7 cars, $40 buses; infield parking an additional $10. No overnight parking or camping in infield, unless approved by Milwaukee Mile for specific event. In camping area, personal vehicles allowed with permits, but not much riding area. No tent camping; no driving stakes into asphalt. No pets; no open fires.
Grandstand: In grandstand, clear plastic bag small enough to fit under seat allowed; camcorder, other personal electronics allowed. No coolers, outside food, or beverages; no folding chairs, umbrellas, or glass; no pets; no noisemakers, horns, or helium balloons.

Mobile Dragway
780 Park Blvd., Irvington, AL 36544
(800) 232-7961
mobiledragway.com
NHRA

Dragway offers 250 free day-parking spaces, 150 free camping spaces. Pit has 150 spaces. Personal vehicles allowed. No glass.

Monadnock Speedway

Rt. 10, Winchester, NH 03470

(603) 239-4067

monadnockspeedway.com

Dodge Weekly

This track did not provide additional information about tailgating or race-day regulations.

Mooresville Speedway

Wilkinson Rd., Mooresville, NC 28115

(704) 663-4685

mooresvilledragway.com

IHRA

Speedway has 30-acre field for free parking. No camping allowed. Personal vehicles fine. No glass or open fires.

Moroso Motorsports Park

17047 Bee Line Hwy. Jupiter, FL 33478

(561) 662-1400

morosomotorsportspark.com

NHRA

Moroso has 5,000 parking spaces inside gates, 10 camping spaces with electric hookups, unlimited dry camping. Electric sites $30 per day; dry sites $15 per day. Campers can arrive, leave when they like. Day parking free. No personal vehicles; alcohol stays in campground. No open fires. Bring bug spray—mosquitoes fierce.

Motor Mile Dragway

6749 Lee Hwy., Radford, VA 24141

(540) 639-1700

motormiledragway.com

IHRA

Dragway has 7,500 free parking spaces. No camping available. Virginia's liquor laws prohibit tailgating.

Motor Mile Speedway
6749 Lee Hwy., Radford, VA 24141

(540) 639-1700

motormilespeedway.com

NASCAR Regional, Dodge Weekly

Speedway shares space, parking with Motor Mile Dragway. No camping available. Virginia's liquor laws prohibit tailgating.

Motordrome Speedway
164 Motordrome Rd., Smithton, PA 15479

(724) 853-7223

motordrome.com

Dodge Weekly

Speedway has unlimited parking. Parking outside gates free; inside gates 30 spots available, $10. No camping available. All personal vehicles allowed. No glass or open fires.

Mountain Park Speedway
718 11th St., Clay City, KY 40312

(606) 663-0369 or (606) 663-2344

mpdragway.com

IHRA

Speedway has 800 feet parking, camping by dragstrip. Parking, camping $10 per event. Personal vehicles allowed. No alcohol—facility in dry county. No open fires.

Muncie Dragway

7901 E. SR 28/67, Albany, IN 47320

(765) 789-8470

munciedrag.com

IHRA

Muncie has 1,500 parking spaces, free with admission. No camping available. All personal vehicles allowed. No glass allowed.

Music City Motorplex

State Fairgrounds

615 State St., Nashville, TN 37204

(765) 789-8470

musiccitymotorplex.com

NASCAR Regional, Dodge Weekly

Motorplex has 7,000 day-parking spaces, separate RV lot for camping. No tent camping. RVs pay $35 for day or overnight parking; other vehicles $3 per day. No golf carts, but other personal vehicles allowed. No glass or open fires.

Music City Raceway

3302 Ivy Point Rd., Goodlettsville, TN 37072

(615) 264-0375

musiccityraceway.com

NHRA

This track did not provide additional information about tailgating or race-day regulations.

Myrtle Beach Speedway

455 Hospitality Lane, Myrtle Beach, SC 29577

(843) 236-0500

myrtlebeachspeedway.com

Dodge Weekly

Speedway has 800 day-parking spaces, plus campground. Day parking $20 for cars, other vehicles. Overnight camping $20, or three days for $35. Personal vehicles okay. No glass or open fires.

Nashville Superspeedway

4847-F McCrary Rd., Lebanon, TN 37090
(866) RACE-TIX
nashvillesuperspeedway.com
Busch Series, Craftsman Truck, IHRA

Superspeedway has room for 15,000 vehicles, but no infield camping. General RV camping $30 for weekend event; limited reserved RV spaces run $160–$280, depending on event and specific site. Reserved RV season pass $700. All-day parking free; day-only RV parking in Lot North 3 only. In camping areas, no hard liquor or wine; no personal motorized vehicles allowed, but bikes okay. No tent camping or pets. Keep flags, other decorations 100 feet from phone, power lines. TVs, stereos, sound systems must stay inside RVs. No scaffolding on top of RVs. Portable scaffolding, trailered platforms forbidden.

National Trail Raceway

2650 National Rd., South West Hebron, OH 43025
(740) 928-5706
nationaltrailraceway.com
NHRA

Raceway has 100 acres day parking. No overnight camping; try campground next door. Parking free for regular events; special events run $5–$20. Shuttles available for large events. Motorcycles, mopeds okay; no ATVs or golf carts. Bicycles okay. No open fires or pets allowed.

Natural Bridge Dragstrip

Dry Well Rd. (Rt. 813), Natural Bridge, VA 24578

(804) 290-0861

IHRA

This track did not provide additional information about tailgating or race-day regulations.

New England Dragway

Rt. 27, PO Box 1320, Epping, NH 03042

(603) 679-8001

newenglanddragway.com

IHRA

Track owner prohibits tailgating or overnight camping by spectators; only race participants may tailgate. Track would not provide any additional information.

New Hampshire International Speedway

1122 Rt. 106 N., Loudon, NH 03307

(603) 783-4931

nhis.com

Nextel Cup, Busch Series, Craftsman Trucks, NASCAR Regional

Camping: No infield camping; day parking free. RV camping $100 per event weekend if purchased before July 1; afterward, camping $125 per event weekend. Park-n-ride shuttles available from Concord to Speedway during Sunday Nextel Cup. Call Greater Concord Chamber of Commerce at (603) 224-2508 for prices. In camping areas, no personal motorized vehicles; no bicycles, pets, or camping tents. Call guest services for current rules on shade canopies, grills, camping furniture, campfires, and departure times. **Grandstand:** In grandstand, fans allowed one cooler up to 14 inches all sides, one clear plastic bag, camera, other personal electronics. No camcorders, glass, bicycles, skateboards, Rollerblades, human transporters, scaffolding, or umbrellas.

New York International Raceway Park

2011 New Rd., Leicester, NY 14481

(585) 382-3030

nyirp.com

IHRA

Park refused to release information on camping, tailgating, or parking. Web site has list of area campgrounds, hotels, etc.

No Problem Raceway Park

6470 Hwy. 996, Bellerose, LA 70346

(985) 369-3692

noproblemraceway.com

NHRA

Park has 120 acres for parking, camping. Day parking included in admission ticket; RV camping $100 for weekend. Personal vehicles okay. Open fires allowed in pits only. No glass allowed.

Northeast Dragway

1099 Lake Rd., Hertford, NC 27944

(252) 264-2066

northeastdragway.com

IHRA

Dragway has 10 acres parking, camping; $10 per day for either. No alcohol or open fires.

Northwest Tennessee Motorsports Park

5469 Hwy. 22, Gleason, TN 38229

(731) 648-9567

northwesttennesseemotorsports.com

NHRA

Park has 500 multiuse spaces available. Camping, day parking cost included in admission. Personal vehicles okay. No glass or open fires.

Norwalk Raceway Park

1300 State Rt. 18, Norwalk, OH 44857

(419) 668-5555

norwalkraceway.com

NHRA

Raceway has 150 acres camping, parking. RVs have 55 sites with hookups available for $75–$150 per weekend, or 100 dry sites for $50–$100 per weekend. Day parking, car camping included in admission. Nearby campground has 450 sites for primitive camping, running $20–$50 per event. No alcohol or glass allowed. Keep open fires contained in pit or ring.

Numidia Dragway

10 Dragstrip Rd., Numidia, PA 17858

(570) 799-5090

numidiadragway.net

NHRA

Dragway has 120 acres for parking, camping. Both included in admission price. Dump station is available. No alcohol or glass allowed. Open fires only in pit area.

Oahe Speedway

28390 Spectators Rd., Pierre, SD 57501

(605) 223-9885

oahespeedway.com

NHRA

Speedway has 50 acres for parking, camping; 55 RV sites offer partial or full hookups. These sites rented only annually, $300–$400 depending on type of hookup. Day, overnight parking for cars included in admission price. No glass.

Oglethorpe Speedway Park

200 Jessup Rd., Porter, GA 31322

(912) 964-8200

ospracing.net

Dodge Weekly

Oglethorpe has 1,000 spaces for vehicles; 20 RV sites with full hookups behind main grandstand. Infield has 200 spaces. RV sites cost $25 first day, $10 per additional day. Rustic camping, day parking, free. No ATVs or golf carts; other personal vehicles okay. No open fires or glass.

Ohio Valley Raceway

632 Katherine Station Rd., West Point, KY 40177

(502) 922-4152

ohiovalleydragway.com

NHRA

Speedway has 50 acres for parking, camping; 55 RV sites offer partial or full hookups.

Raceway has 500 day-parking spots, no overnight camping. Most parking free; parking in pits $2. No open fires or glass. Tailgate all day; leave by midnight.

Old Bridge Township Raceway Park

230 Pension Rd., Englishtown, NJ 07726

(732) 446-7800

etownraceway.com

NHRA

Park has 5,000 free day-parking spaces, no overnight camping. Arrive and tailgate from daybreak up to race time; leave when race is done. No open fires or glass.

Old Dominion Speedway

10611 Dumfries Rd., Manassas, VA 20112

(703) 361-7753

olddominionspeedway.com

Dodge Weekly

Speedway has 15 acres multiuse parking. Parking, camping free. Personal vehicles allowed for licensed drivers. No open fires or glass. No security presence on Wednesdays.

Orangeburg Dragstrip

Dragstrip Rd., Orangeburg, SC 29115

(803) 534-8322

orangeburgdragstrip.com

IHRA

This track did not provide additional information about tailgating or race-day regulations.

O'Reilly Raceway Park at Indianapolis

10267 E. U.S. Hwy. 136, Indianapolis, IN 46234

(317) 291-4090

oreillyracewaypark.com

Busch Series, Craftsman Trucks, NHRA

O'Reilly offers no camping on property. Day parking runs $10 per day, $25 for weekend pass. For RV camping, contact Raceview Family Campground next door to track—200 spaces available with electric hookups. Raceview also offers day parking, $10–$20 depending on event. Adult camping rates are $15 per person, per day, with some discounts for seven- or eight-day stays; teens 13 to 15 years half price; children under 12 free. Electric hookup $18 per day. See raceviewcampground.com for camping rules. Note: For NASCAR Speedfest, NHRA Nationals events only, O'Reilly provides 60 RV sites, $100 for event; call for arrival times. At O'Reilly campsite, no pets, tent camping, or glass; no personal motorized vehicles.

Orlando Speed World Dragway

19442 E. Colonial Dr., Orlando, FL 32820

(407) 568-5522

speedworlddragway.com

NHRA

Dragway has 1,000 day-parking spaces; no overnight camping. Parking included in admission price. No open fires or glass.

Osceola Dragway

56328 Ash Rd., Osceola, IN 46561

(574) 674-8400

osceoladragway.com

IHRA

Dragstrip has 20 acres of day parking; no overnight camping. No alcohol or pets allowed.

Outer Banks Speedway

426 Venson Rd., Creswell, NC 27928

(252) 797-RACE

outerbanksspeedway.com

IHRA

Speedway has 2,500 multiuse parking spaces. Primitive/dry camping only. Usage fee included in admission price. No open fires.

Oxford Dragway

29 Oxford Homes Lane, Oxford, ME 04270

(207) 268-2217

oxforddragway.com

IHRA

Oxford has 1,000 event parking spaces, Thursday through Saturday only; no overnight camping. Personal vehicles okay. No glass allowed.

Ozark International Raceway

Highway U, Rogersville, MO 65742

(417) 738-2222

ozarkdragstrip.com

IHRA

This track is new to the IHRA lineup. No information was available by press time. Please call phone number for information.

Pacemakers Dragway Park

8926 Columbus Rd., Mt. Vernon, OH 43050

(740) 397-2720

pacemakersdragway.com

NHRA

Park has 1,500 camping, parking spaces Friday through Sunday. Both included in admission fee. No glass allowed. Keep open fires contained.

Pacific Raceways

13001 114th Ave. S., Ken, WA 98042

(253) 639-5927

pacificraceways.com

NHRA

Raceway has room for more than 10,000 vehicles. Overnight camping allowed on multiday special events only. Camping prices vary from event to event. Parking included in admission price. Fans arrive 3 p.m.; leave 1 hour after race's end. No alcohol, grills, or open fires permitted.

Paris Dragstrip

4369 U.S. Hwy. 82 E., Paris, TX 75462

(903) 737-0410

parisdragstrip.com

NHRA

Dragstrip has room for more than 250 vehicles. Camping, parking included in admission. No open fires or glass allowed.

Peoria Speedway

3520 W. Farmington Rd., Peoria, IL 61604

(309) 673-3342

peoriaspeedway.com

Dodge Weekly

Speedway has 1,500 spaces for vehicles. Camping during special events only. When camping available, campers can arrive day before race. Parking, camping included in admission. No decorations, alcohol, or grills; no open fires allowed.

Phoenix International Raceway

7602 S. Avondale Blvd., Avondale, AZ 85323

(623) 463-5400

phoenixraceway.com

Nextel Cup, Busch Series, Craftsman Trucks, NASCAR Regional

Camping: Raceway has 38,000 day-parking spaces, 6,000 camping sites; no infield camping. All day parking free; RVs can use day parking Sunday only. Camping runs $40–$150 depending on site. In camping, tailgating areas, grills okay unless weather conditions prohibit all fires. No campfires or personal motorized vehicles allowed; no driving stakes into asphalt. Most decorations okay, but not inflatable blimps. No water balloon launchers or scaffolding. Respect quiet hours. **Grandstand:** In grandstand, fans allowed one soft-sided cooler or bag up to 6 x 6 x 12 inches, and one clear plastic bag up to 18 x 18 x 4 inches; seat cushions, camcorders, other personal electronics allowed. No alcohol, glass, oversized bags or coolers, hard-sided coolers, thermoses, or insulated cups; no hollow-tube construction seat cushions or umbrellas; no strollers, wagons, bicycles, golf carts, or ATVs; no pets.

Piedmont Dragway

6750 Holts Store Rd., Julia, NC 37283

(336) 449-7411

piedmontdragway.com

IHRA

Dragway has 4,000 spaces for camping, day parking. Price included in admission fee. Dump station available. No open fires, glass, or pets allowed.

Pine Valley Raceway Park

3427 FM 2497, Lufkin, TX 75904

(936) 699-3227

pinevalleyracing.com

IHRA

Park has 10 acres all-purpose camping, parking. Price included in admission fee. Campers leave by noon on day after event. No open fires or glass.

Pittsburgh Raceway Park

538 Stone Jug Rd., New Alexandria, PA 15670

(412) 951-4161

pittsburghracewaypark.com

IHRA

Park has 1,000 multiuse parking spaces. Camping, parking included in admission fee. No hookups available. No open fires or glass. All campers, spectators must leave by midnight after end of race.

Pocono Raceway

Long Pond Rd., Long Pond, PA 18334

(800) RACEWAY (1-800-722-3929)

poconoraceway.com

Nextel Cup

Camping: Camping runs $40–$500, depending on location and length of stay; race tickets not included. Day parking free; most parking, camping in grass areas. In camping areas, no personal motorized vehicles; no tent camping. Tailgaters must store shade canopies before entering grandstand; campers must do same during racing. Alcohol okay, but no kegs or beer balls. No external TVs or amplified music. No pets, open fires, balloons, or kites. **Grandstand:** In grandstand, fans allowed coolers up to 12 x 12 inches. Backpacks, fanny packs, plastic bags also okay. Camcorders, other personal electronics allowed. No glass, objects obstructing others' view of track, or items posing safety or health risk.

Portland International Raceway

West Delta Park

1940 N. Victory Blvd., Portland, OR 97217

(503) 823-7223

portlandraceway.com

NHRA, Champ Car

Raceway has 1,500 all-purpose vehicle spaces. Parking, camping both included in admission fee. More spaces available outside gates. No open fires or glass. All camping primitive.

Pueblo Motorsports Park

3733 N. Pueblo Blvd., Pueblo, CO 81008

(719) 583-0907

pueblomotorsportspark.com

NHRA

Park has 1,000 free parking, camping spaces. No hookups available. No open fires or glass allowed.

Quaker City Raceway

10359 W. Southrange Rd., Salem, OH 44460

(330) 332-5335

quakercityraceway.com

IHRA

Raceway has 5,000 parking, camping spaces. Day parking free; camping $10 per day with electric hookup. All personal vehicles allowed. No open fires. If supplies are needed, convenience store only 1 mile away, Wal-Mart within 5 miles.

Raceway Park

1 Checkered Flag Blvd., Shakopee, MN 55379

(952) 445-2257

NASCAR Regional, Dodge Weekly

Park has 5 acres for parking only; no camping. Parking included in admission fee. Personal vehicles allowed. No glass, open fires, or pets.

Red River Raceway

13500 Gilliam-Scott's Slough, Gilliam, LA 71029

(903) 571-7137

redriverraceway.net

NHRA

Raceway has 1,000 multiuse spaces. Parking, camping included in admission fee. No glass allowed, but open fires okay. Convenience store 3 miles from track.

Redding Dragstrip

Desperado Trail, Redding, CA 96002

(530) 221-1311

reddingdragstrip.net

NHRA

Dragstrip has 100 acres parking, camping. Price included in admission. Campers can arrive a day early; all must leave 1 hour after race's end. No open fires or alcohol allowed.

Redline Raceway

Bailey Corners Rd., Granville Summit, PA 16926

(903) 527-5911

redlineraceway.com

IHRA

Raceway has 2,000 parking, dry-camping spaces. Price included in admission. No glass allowed; open fires okay.

Renegade Raceways

1395 Track Rd., Wapato, WA 98951

(509) 877-4621

renegaderaceway.com

NHRA

This track did not provide additional information about tailgating or race-day regulations.

Richmond Dragway

1955 Portugee Rd., Sandstone, VA 23150

(804) 737-1193

richmonddragway.com

IHRA

Dragway has 1,000 paved parking spots, room for 2,000 more in grass lot. No overnight camping. Parking included in admission fee. No open fires.

Richmond International Raceway

600 E. Laburnum Ave., Richmond, VA 23222

(866) 455-RACE or (888) 472-2849

rir.com

Nextel Cup, Busch Series, IRL

Camping: RIR's camping areas have 12- to 15-year waiting list for new campers. Camping runs $175–$275 per event. Nearby campgrounds include Azalea Flea Market, (804) 329-8853; Americamp, (800) 628-2802. Day parking free. On-site shuttles free; off-site shuttles $5. In camping areas, banners, flags no higher than vehicle. Pets must be leashed. External TVs, amplified music okay, but respect quiet times. Tailgaters must tailgate in front of or behind vehicle; keep everything inside space. **Grandstand:** Fans allowed one soft-sided cooler or bag up to 6 x 6 x 12 inches, one clear plastic bag up to 18 x 18 x 4 inches; seat cushions, camcorder, other personal electronics all fine. No hard-sided coolers, insulated cups, or thermoses; no glass, strollers, umbrellas, or folding chairs; no pets; no oversized bags or backpacks. Note: Track is located within Richmond city limits, with nearby hotels, stores, other campgrounds.

Riverhead Raceway

CR 58, Riverhead, NY 11901

(631) 842-7223

riverheadraceway.com

NASCAR Regional, Dodge Weekly

Raceway has 500 day-parking spaces. No camping available. Arrive as early as 3 hours before race; leave 1 hour after race's end. No grills, alcohol, or open fires allowed. No pets.

Road America

N7390 Hwy. 67, Elkhart Lake, WI 53020

(800) 465-7223

roadamerica.com

Champ Car

Road America has 628 acres for camping, parking. Campers arrive as early as Thursday before races. All depart 30 minutes after event's end. General tent, RV camping $75 for multiday event. Reserved RV camping $275 for multiday event. Infield day parking $25; other parking free. All must buy general weekend ticket. No unlicensed personal vehicles or ATVs allowed. Facility rents golf carts. Keep shade canopies 10 x 10 feet. No loud music or extensive/professional sound systems. Respect quiet hours. Open fire in patio fire pit okay; no ground fires. Extinguish coals thoroughly. Advance permission required for pets.

Rock Falls Raceway

1000th St., Rock Falls, WI 54755

(715) 879-5089

rockfallsraceway.com

NHRA

Raceway has 500 day-parking spaces. No camping overnight. Parking included in admission fee. Open fires okay; no glass allowed.

Rockford Speedway

9572 Forest Hills Rd., Loves Park, IL 61111

(815) 633-0735

rockfordspeedway.com

Dodge Weekly

Speedway has 20 acres multiuse parking. Overnight parking allowed in parking lot. More camping at Rock Cut State Park, several other campgrounds. Contact Rockford Area Convention & Visitors Bureau for information, (800) 521-0849 or gorockford.com. VIP parking $2; other parking free. No glass or open fires.

Rockingham Dragway

2153 U.S. Hwy. 1 N., Rockingham, NC 28379

(910) 582-3400

rockinghamdragway.com

IHRA

Dragway has 1,500 parking, camping sites. Inside gates, 24 RV sites with hookups; outside, 44 sites with hookups. Day parking free; camping runs $30–$100 depending on location. Dry camping free. No open fires, pets, or glass allowed.

Rocky Mountain Raceways

6555 W. 2100 S., West Valley City, UT 84128

(801) 252-9557

rmrracing.com

Dodge Weekly, NHRA

Raceway has more than 2,000 parking, camping sites. Price included in admission fee. Web site has additional campground info. No open fires.

Rolling Thunder Dragstrip
19340 Jesup Ave., Pacific Junction, IA 51561
(727) 573-9700
midamericamotorplex.com
NHRA

Dragstrip has more than 50 acres camping, parking. Day parking included in admission fee. Camping $25 per weekend. No hookups, but showers available. All spectators arrive noon race day; campers can stay overnight. No open fires or glass.

Route 66 Raceway
3200 S. Chicago St., Joliet, IL 60436
(815) 727-7223
route66raceway.com
NHRA

Raceway is on Chicagoland Speedway property and shares all parking, camping. There's lots of it, too. During NHRA National event weekends, day parking $5, camping $400 with electric hookups, $300 without. During these events, fans must purchase event tickets with motorhome parking. No personal vehicles, glass, or public intoxication. Open fires okay in enclosed, off-ground containers. Decorations, flags must be lower than RV rooflines. (For more, see **Chicagoland Speedway** entry.)

Roxboro Motorsports Dragway

1452 Thomas Store Rd., Timberlake, NC 27583

(336) 364-3724

roxboromotorsports.com

IHRA

Dragway has more than 2,000 all-purpose parking spaces. Campers arrive day before race, stay until day after. Day-trippers leave by midnight. Parking, camping included in admission fee. Open fires okay.

Sacramento Raceway Park

5305 Excelsior Rd., Sacramento, CA 95827

(916) 363-2653

sacramentoraceway.com

NHRA

Park has more than 2,000 day-parking spaces; no overnight camping. All parking free. No open fires or pets; otherwise, everything pretty much okay. Supermarket, stores nearby.

Samoa Dragstrip

Lincoln Ave., Samoa, CA 95564

(707) 443-5203

samoadragstrip.com

NHRA

Dragstrip has more than 250 camping, parking sites. Personal vehicles okay. No skateboards allowed on facility property. No alcohol in pit area. No glass or open fires.

San Antonio Raceway

3641 S. Santa Clara Rd., Marion, TX 78124

(210) 698-2310

sanantonioraceway.com

IHRA

Raceway has 15 acres parking, holds up to 10,000 vehicles. Special-event RV camping $100 per weekend; all other parking free. One hundred camping sites, 40 RV parking spaces available. No open fires or glass. Web site has good area guide.

San Antonio Speedway

14901 State Hwy. 16 S., San Antonio, TX 78264

(210) 628-1499

sanantoniospeedway.com

Dodge Weekly

Speedway has more than 20 acres parking, camping. Both included in admission fee. All camping primitive. No open fires or glass. Speedway only asphalt half-mile track in Texas.

Shasta Raceway Park

1890 Briggs St., Anderson, CA 96007

(530) 378-6789

shastaracewaypark.org

NASCAR Regional, Dodge Weekly

Park has 1,400 parking, camping spaces. Additional parking available at Shasta District Fairgrounds. Camping $10 inside gate; no charge in lot outside. No open fires, glass, or pets.

Silver Dollar Raceway

Hwy. 46 W., Reynolds, GA 31076

(478) 847-4414

silverdollarraceway.com

NHRA

Raceway has 30 acres parking, camping; both included in admission fee. No open fires or glass. Dump station available. Web site has extensive listing of area motels.

Skyview Dragstrip

114 Skyline Dr., Tioga Center, NY 13845

(607) 687-9392

skyviewdrags.com

IHRA

Dragstrip has room for 4,000 vehicles, day parking included in admission fee. Campers have 70 pit spaces with hookups sold by season only, $175–$225. No open fires or glass.

Sooner Motorplex

11042 SW Sheridan Rd., Lawton, OK 73505

(580) 695-9648

soonermotorplex.com

IHRA

Motorplex has 3,000 camping, parking spaces. Day-trip tailgaters arrive 5 p.m., leave 1 hour after race's conclusion. Campers come day before race, leave day after. No recreational driving of personal vehicles. No open fires or glass.

South Boston Speedway

1188 James D. Hagood Hwy., South Boston, VA 24592

(434) 572-4947

southbostonspeedway.com

NASCAR Regional, Dodge Weekly

This track did not provide additional information about tailgating or race-day regulations.

South Georgia Motorsports Park

2521 Hwy. 41 N., Cecil, GA 31627

(229) 896-7000

sgmpracing.com

NHRA

Park has 4,000 free parking spaces. No overnight camping available. Tailgaters come 2 hours before race starts, leave 1 hour after race ends. No open fires or glass allowed. No one under 14 years allowed in speedway pit area.

South Mountain Dragway

Petersburg Rd., Boiling Springs, PA 17007

(717) 258-6287

southmountaindragway.us

NHRA

Dragway has 1,500 spots for vehicles. All camping, parking free. No glass or open fires.

Southern National Raceway Park

8071 Newsome Mill Rd., Lucama, NC 27851

(919) 284-1114

southernnational.net

NASCAR Regional, Dodge Weekly

Facility has room for more than 5,000 vehicles, with 149 trackside spaces reserved for season pass holders. Trackside spots run $450–$550. No glass at track; pets must be leashed.

Southwestern International Speedway

11300 South Houghton Rd., Tucson, AZ 85747

(520) 762-9700

sirace.com

NHRA

Raceway has 3,000 parking spaces, but no camping. More than 50 motels available within 20 minutes of track. Tailgaters arrive 8 a.m., clear out by midnight. All parking free. No glass allowed. Open fires okay.

Speedworld Raceway Park

19421 W. Jomax Rd., Wittman, AZ 85361

 (623) 388-2424

speedworldmotorplex.com

NHRA

Park has 3,000 day-parking spaces. No overnight parking available. Fans can arrive at noon, must depart 1 hour after end of race. Park doesn't allow alcohol or glass; otherwise, no real restrictions. Watch open fires—Arizona's awfully dry.

Spencer Speedway

3011 Ridge Rd. (Rt. 104), Williamson, NY 14589

(315) 589-3018

spencer-speedway.com

Dodge Weekly

Speedway has 2,000 day-parking spaces. No overnight parking available. Tailgaters can arrive 1 hour before race, leave 1 hour after race ends. No glass allowed. Open fires must be contained in fire pits or rings.

SRCA Dragstrip

4555 W. Barton County Rd., Great Bend, KS 67539

(785) 483-1980

srcadragstrip.com

NHRA

Dragstrip has 1,000 paved parking spots, plus room for more than 2,000 more in grass lot. Personal vehicles allowed only in pit and staging areas. SRCA leases 6 acres to neighboring armory; this area off-limits to vehicles. No open fires or glass.

Stafford Motor Speedway

55 West St., Stafford Springs, CT 06076

(860) 684-2783

staffordmotorspeedway.com

NASCAR Regional, Dodge Weekly

Speedway has 4,000 paved spaces for tailgaters, campers. Both parking and camping free. Overnight parking area opens by 8 a.m. on scheduled event day. No ATV's, dirt bikes, or mopeds on Speedway grounds. Golf carts permitted, if registered with speedway office; must provide proof of insurance. Open fires permitted only in pit or fire ring.

Star Speedway

176 Exeter Rd., Epping, NH 03042

(603) 679-5306

starspeedway.com

Dodge Weekly

Speedway can accommodate 3,000 vehicles, day parking only. Parking free. Personal vehicles okay. No open fires or glass. No unruly behavior or public intoxication.

State Capitol Dragway

11436 Hwy. 190 W., Port Allen, LA 70767

(225) 627-4574

statecapitoldragway.com

NHRA

This track did not provide additional information about tailgating or race-day regulations.

Sturgis Dragway

SD-79, Sturgis, SD 57785

(605) 347-1301

sturgisdrags.com

NHRA

Dragway can hold 1,500 vehicles. Tailgaters may arrive 8 a.m., leave 1 hour after end of race. Personal vehicles okay.

Sumerduck Dragway

14027 Royalls Mill Rd., Sumerduck, VA 22742

(540) 845-1656

sumerduckdragway.com

IHRA

Dragway has 500 parking spaces, plus 30 RV spots, all free. No open fires or glass allowed. Personal vehicles okay. Family-oriented atmosphere. No obnoxious behavior allowed.

Sunshine Dragstrip

4398 126th Ave., Clearwater, FL 33762

(727) 573-9700

sunshinedragstrip.com

NHRA

Dragstrip has room for 2,000 vehicles. No overnight camping; day parking only, all free. No open fires or glass allowed. Otherwise, Sunshine's a pretty easygoing place. Personal vehicles okay.

Talladega Superspeedway

3366 Speedway Blvd., Talladega, AL 35160

(877) Go2-DEGA; (877) 462-3342

talladegasuperspeedway.com

Nextel Cup, Busch Series, Craftsman Trucks

Camping: Talladega has 1,200 acres for camping, including infield. RV camping prices run $60–$1,550 for event. Smaller camping vehicles, tent camping $245–$285 depending on length of stay. Three free camping areas available: Free West C, Free North Park, Free Family. Day car parking free. In camping areas, no personal motorized vehicles or bikes; no external sound systems. Small open or wood fires allowed in contained fire rings. No pets. Quiet time enforced midnight to 6 a.m. **Grandstand:** In grandstand, fans allowed one soft-sided cooler or insulated bag up to 6 x 6 x 12 inches, one clear plastic bag up to 18 x 18 x 4 inches. Camcorders, other personal electronic items allowed. No glass, umbrellas, folding chairs, baby seats, or strollers; no pets, bicycles, or Rollerblades. Don't stand in seats. Children 11 years and under allowed into general admission grandstand free with paying adult Thursday (if event scheduled), Friday, Saturday. All ages must have valid grandstand ticket for Sunday Nextel Cup race.

Team Possibilities Jr. Raceway

Qualcomm Stadium, Southwest Parking Lot
9449 Friars Rd., San Diego, CA 92108
(619) 390-1332
teampossibilities.com
NHRA

Raceway has 100 parking spaces available, with overnight camping night before race. Spectators, participants should be gone 2 hours after race ends. Only licensed drivers operate motorized vehicles (except participating Junior Dragsters). Helmets required if riding non-motorized vehicles.

Temple Raceway

13550 Hwy. 95, Little River, TX 76534
(254) 982-4512
templeacademy.com
IHRA
This track did not provide additional information about tailgating or race-day regulations.

Texas Motor Speedway

3545 Lone Star Circle, Ft. Worth, TX 76177

(817) 215-8500

texasmotorspeedway.com

Nextel Cup, Busch Series, Craftsman Trucks

Camping: Speedway has 5,700 RV campsites, 1,100 tent campsites, 1,000 infield sites (only available for Nextel Cup events). Day parking, including buses, totals 553,700 spaces. Camping prices vary greatly, from $50 for unreserved spots to $2,000 for top infield sites. Most day parking free; reserved parking runs $20–$75 depending on day and event. In camping areas, personal motorized vehicles not allowed; bicycles okay. No grilling during practice times or race activity; otherwise, grills fine. Keep pets on a leash. No cruising permitted in camping areas. No flatbed trailers (over 10 feet long) or box trucks allowed in campgrounds. City noise ordinance enforced—obey quiet hours guidelines. Note: During cup events, Speedway offers on-site campground grocery store. **Grandstand:** In grandstand, fans allowed one bag, plus one cooler, both up to 14 inches all sides. Camcorders, other personal electronics okay. No glass; no oversized bags or coolers; no umbrellas; no strollers, skateboards, scooters, or Rollerblades.

Texas Motorplex

7500 W. Hwy. 287, Ennis, TX 75119

(972) 878-2641

texasmotorplex.com

NHRA

Motorplex has 20,000 parking spaces, plus 4,000 for special events. All are free during O'Reilly Fall Nationals. At other events, a small fee may be charged. RVs can park in day spaces, but not overnight. Self-contained RVs camp overnight one to four days in Texas Motorplex Campground Park, one spot per RV. Price can be $60, or track may offer spaces for free. Motorhome Corral has trackside RV parking for $600 per event. No personal vehicles in campground or parking lot. No glass, open fires, or pets.

Texas Raceway

3830 New Hope Rd., Kennedale, TX 76060

(817) 483-0356

texasraceway.com

NHRA

Raceway has 30 acres of free day parking. No overnight camping available. Personal vehicles allowed. No open fires or glass.

Thompson International Speedway

205 E. Thompson Rd., Thompson, CT 06277

(860) 923-228

thompsonspeedway.com

NASCAR Regional, Dodge Weekly

Speedway has 500 parking spaces, plus 30 slots for RVs. All camping dry; no hookups. No glass, open fires, or pets at speedway. Personal vehicles okay.

Thompson Raceway Park

8233 Sidley Rd., Thompson, OH 44086

(216) 251-5200

thompsonracewaypark.com

NHRA

Park has more than 3,000 spaces for vehicles. Overnight camping available. Both overnight and day parking free. Day-trippers arrive when gates open between 8 and 10 a.m. depending on event; leave by 5 p.m. No glass allowed.

Thunder Hill Raceway

24801 IH-35, Kyle, TX 78640

(512) 262-1352

thunderhillraceway.com

NASCAR Regional

Raceway has more than 3,000 day-parking spaces, no overnight camping. RVs have separate lot. All parking free. No glass allowed. Personal vehicles okay.

Thunder Valley Dragway

450th Ave., Marion, SD 57043

(605) 648-3604

thundervalleydragways.com

IHRA

Dragway has 500 acres for camping, parking. Day parking free. Camping runs from $10 for unreserved dry sites to $300 for season-pass site on first row, with electric hookup. No open fires or glass.

Thunder Valley Raceway Park

10500 S. 48th St., Lexington, OK 73051

(405) 872-3429

okthunder.com

NHRA

Park has room for 2,000 vehicle spaces. Day parking, camping both free. No open fires or glass allowed.

Top Gun Raceway
Schurz Hwy. (U.S. 95), Fallon, NV 89406
(800) 325-7448
topgunraceway.com
NHRA

Raceway can accommodate 3,000 vehicles. No overnight camping available; all day parking free. Track forbids glass products. No alcohol allowed in pit area.

Tri-State Dragway
2362 Hamilton-Cleves Rd., Hamilton, OH 45013
(513) 863-0562
tristatedragway.com
IHRA

Dragway has more than 1,000 camping, parking spaces, all free. No glass or open fires. Don't dump oil in trashcans or waste water on ground. Make sure all trash and litter is picked up.

Tri-State Raceway
2217 270th Ave., Earlville, IA 52041
(563) 923-3724
tristateraceway.com
NHRA

Raceway has more than 1,000 free day-parking spaces for vehicles. RVs park at neighboring campground a few hundred yards away. Campground has 100 sites with full hookups at $20 per day, $125 per week. Tent camping $10 per day. No open fires or glass at track or campground. Pets allowed in campground only.

Tucson Raceway Park
12500 S. Houghton Rd., Tucson, AZ 85747
(520) 762-9200
tucsonracewaypark.com
Dodge Weekly
This track did not provide additional information about tailgating or race-day regulations.

Tulsa Raceway Park
3101 N. Garnett Rd., Tulsa, OK 74116
(918) 437-RACE
tulsaracewaypark.com
IHRA

Park has more than 5,000 spaces for vehicles, but none for overnight camping. Parking free. Personal vehicles only allowed as tow vehicles or for activities related to racing. No recreational use permitted. No open fires or glass at facility.

Twin City Dragway
3695 Prairie Rd., Monroe, LA 71201
(318) 387-8563
twincitydragway.com
NHRA

Dragway has more than 3,000 parking, camping spaces, all free. Campers stay night of race, leave next day. Personal vehicles for crew, staff use only; no joyriding permitted. No bicycles or scooters allowed. No glass on facility property.

Twin State Speedway

Thrasher Rd., Claremont, NH 03743

(603) 543-3106

twinstatespeedway.net

Dodge Weekly

Speedway (formerly Claremont Speedway) has 4,000 free vehicle spaces for parking, camping. Track prohibits glass. Atmosphere friendly, family-oriented.

US 13 Dragway

Sussex Hwy. (Rt. 13), Delmar, DE 19956

(302) 875-1911

delawareracing.com

NHRA

Dragway is part of Delaware Motorsports Complex, with more than 30 acres for parking, camping. Campers stay night of race, leave next day. Parking, camping included in admission fee. All personal vehicles must be registered with track.

US 19 Dragway

1304 Williamsburg Rd., Albany, GA 31705

(229) 431-0077

us19dragway.com

NHRA

Dragway has more than 2,500 free day-parking spaces. No overnight camping. No open fires or glass allowed at facility.

US 41 Dragway
2695 W. 50 S., Morocco, IN 47963
(219) 285-2200
us41dragway.com
IHRA

Dragway has more than 3,000 free day-parking spaces. Racers can camp overnight, but not spectators. No open fires or glass at track.

US 131 Motorsports Park
1249 12th St., Martin, MI 49070
(269) 672-7800
us131motorsportspark.com
IHRA

Park has 1,000 day-parking spaces for vehicles. Campers can choose between three camp-grounds, all within 10 miles of track—Schnable Lake Campground, Miller Lake Campground, or Hidden Ridge RV Community. No glass allowed on park property.

Virginia Motorsports Park
8018 Boydton Plank Rd., Petersburg, VA 23803
(804) 862-3174
virginiamotorsportspk.com
NHRA

Facility covers 700 acres with more than 10,000 parking spaces. Day parking free. Day parking also available for up to 130 motorhomes, no charge. Overnight camping available at Campton Campground nearby. No open fires or glass allowed. Drivers of any wheeled vehicle must be licensed, 16 years or older.

Wabash Valley Dragway

Wabash Valley Fairgrounds

3801 S. U.S. Hwy. 41, Terre Haute, IN 47802

(812) 232-7223

wabashvalleydragway.com

NHRA

Dragway has 5,000 day-parking spaces; no camping. Parking free. Personal vehicles okay; skateboards prohibited. No glass or open fires.

Wall Township Speedway

1803 State Rt. 34, Wall Township, NJ 07719

(732) 681-6400

wallspeedway.com

Dodge Weekly

Speedway has 5,000 free, day-parking spaces. No overnight parking. No open fires or glass. Alcohol restricted to spectator parking areas.

Ware Shoals Dragway

17052 Hwy. 25, Ware Shoals, SC 29692

(864) 861-2467

wareshoalsdragway.com

IHRA

Dragway has more than 5,000 free day-parking spaces. No overnight camping. No glass or open fires.

Waterford Speedbowl

1080 Hartford Turnpike, Waterford, CT 06385

(860) 442-1585

speedbowl.com

NASCAR Regional, Dodge Weekly

Speedbowl has 2,000 free day-parking spaces. No overnight camping. Guests may not use grills, have open fires, or consume alcohol on property.

Watkins Glen International

2790 County Rt. 16, Watkins Glen, NY 14891

(866) 4611-RACE (7223)

theglen.com

Nextel Cup, Busch Series, IRL

Camping: The Glen offers 2,431 reserved camping spaces, plus more unreserved camping. Day parking covers over 2,000 acres, all free. Overnight parking available for $25–$40 during Nextel Cup, Grand Prix weekends. Advance-purchase camping runs $64–$200, full price $75–$225. General admission tickets required for anyone camping, includes infield access. In camping areas, no personal motorized vehicles; no bikes during Nextel Cup or Grand Prix. Canopy must be under 20 x 20 feet; no circus or party tents. Ask before bringing oversized grills. Campfires okay. No cargo vehicles or trailers. Professionally modified school buses with permanent cooking, sanitary facilities okay. Scaffolding limited to one section, 6 feet high. Canopies in Tailgate Zone areas must stay lower than vehicles during on-track activity.

Grandstand: In grandstand, fans allowed one soft-sided cooler or bag up to 6 x 6 x 12 inches, one clear plastic bag up to 18 x 18 x 4 inches. Seat cushions, camcorders, other personal electronics allowed. No hard-sided coolers, thermoses, or insulated cups; no strollers, umbrellas, oversized bags, or backpacks. Children's wristbands available. Garage wristbands available for Grand Prix weekend $40; no clothing, age restrictions—minors must be with adult.

Wenatchee Valley's Super Oval
Fancher Field Rd., East Wenatchee, WA 98802
(509) 884-8592
wvso.com
NASCAR Regional

Wenatchee has capacity for 10,000 vehicles. No overnight camping; day parking free. Personal vehicles may be driven in parking lots, but not inside racetrack gates. Chelan County has six state or local parks with camping facilities nearby. No glass or open fires.

Western Colorado Dragway
115 32 Rd., Grand Junction, CO 81503
(970) 487-3236; on race days (970) 243-9022
western-colorado-dragway.com
NHRA

Dragway has many acres of parking—they've never run out. No overnight camping, but two RV parks nearby. Gate fee $5 on Friday, $6 on Saturday for all vehicles. Call track before bringing personal vehicles or pets. Spectators should dress for "high desert" conditions; temperatures very hot during day, but chilly after sunset. Kids have sand pit play area next to grandstand.

Wichita International Raceway
7800 61st N., Maize, KS 67101
(316) 729-4448
teamwir.com
NHRA

Raceway has 2,000 free parking, camping spaces. Open fires must be contained in approved fire pit or fire ring.

Wichita Raceway Park

1633 FM 369 N., Iowa Park, TX 76367

(940) 592-1069

wichitaracewaypark.com

NHRA

Park has more than 4,000 spaces for parking, camping, all free. Personal vehicles may only be used by track management or race crews in pit area, never for recreational use. Spectators may use personal vehicles in parking lots only. No glass.

Wilkesboro Raceway Park

726 Dragway Rd., Wilkesboro, NC 28697

(336) 973-7223

wilkesbororacewaypark.com

IHRA

Park has 5,000 free day-parking spaces; no overnight camping. Personal vehicles allowed for pit use only. No glass or open fires.

Windy Hollow Dragway

Windy Hollow Rd., Owensboro, KY 42301

(270) 785-4300

windyhollowdragway.com

NHRA

Dragway has 3,000 free parking, camping spaces. No glass allowed.

Wisconsin International Raceway

W1460 County Rd. KK, Kaukauna, WI 54130

(920) 759-7456

wirracing.com

IHRA

Raceway can accommodate 3,000 vehicles for parking, camping; all included in admission fee. No hookups available for campers. No glass or open fires.

Woodburn Dragstrip

7730 Hwy. 219, Woodburn, OR 97071

(503) 982-4461

woodburndragstrip.com

NHRA

Dragstrip has 50 acres parking, camping. Campsites (all primitive) practically unlimited. Campers arrive day before event, leave directly after event ends. Sixty-five VIP camping spaces available (must be reserved) for $25. Overnight parking $10 for cars. No open fires or glass at track.

Yakima Speedway
1600 Pacific Ave., Yakima, WA 98901
(509) 248-0647
yakimaspeedway.us
NASCAR Regional

Speedway has 5,000 day-parking spaces. No camping available. No barbecues or open flame containers for cooking. No pets; no glass.

Yellowstone Dragstrip
8405 Raceway Lane, Acton, MT 59002
(406) 669-3300
yellowstonedragstrip.com
NHRA

Dragstrip has 14 acres of paved pit parking, with unlimited, unpaved overflow parking. No overnight camping, parking. Personal vehicles okay. No fires of any kind, including barbecue grills, without permit from general manager. No glass allowed at track.Win a trip to Miami and the final race of the season!

Win a trip to Miami

and the **final race of the season!**

It's easy—just go to **theultimatetailgater.com/racing** and enter to win a trip for two to Miami, including tickets to the Nextel Cup race at the Homestead-Miami Speedway in November!

Enter now at theultimatetailgater.com/racing!

Sponsored by

FANHUB.COM

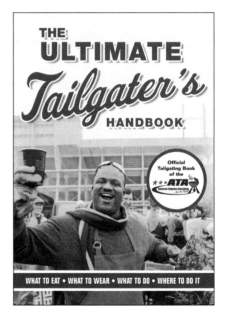

The Ultimate Tailgater's Travel Guide: More Than 20 Great Road Trips will help you tailgate on the road like a local! Filled with tips for tailgating and inside information on RV parks, hotels, restaurants, and city attractions, this book will help you plan a great road trip to cities from Seattle to New York. After all, you're in town for a few days and want to do something after the parking lot clears.

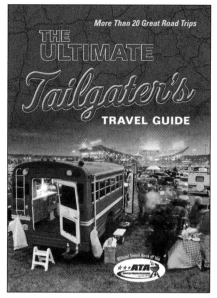

Also at **theultimatetailgater.com**, you'll find tailgating videos and podcasts, contests, and more!

For everything you need to know about the centerpiece of your tailgate party—the food—visit theultimatetailgatechef.com. You'll find recipes, cooking videos, podcasts, and more!